Lecture Notes in Computer Science 8601

Commenced Publication in 1973
Founding and Former Series Editors:
Gerhard Goos, Juris Hartmanis, and Jan van Leeuwen

T0254752

Juan Romero   James McDermott
João Correia (Eds.)

Evolutionary and Biologically Inspired Music, Sound, Art and Design

Third International Conference, EvoMUSART 2014
Granada, Spain, April 23-25, 2014
Revised Selected Papers

Springer

Volume Editors

Juan Romero
University of A Coruña, School of Computer Science
Department of Communications and Information Technologies
Campus de Elviña, 15071 A Coruña, Spain
E-mail: jj@udc.es

James McDermott
University College Dublin
Complex and Adaptive Systems Laboratory
Lochlann Quinn School of Business
Donnybrook, Dublin 4, Ireland
E-mail: jmmcd@jmmcd.net

João Correia
University of Coimbra, CISUC
Department of Informatics Engineering
Pinhal de Marrocos, 3030 Coimbra, Portugal
E-mail: jncor@dei.uc.pt

Cover illustration designed by Laura Pirovano.

ISSN 0302-9743   e-ISSN 1611-3349
ISBN 978-3-662-44334-7   e-ISBN 978-3-662-44335-4
DOI 10.1007/978-3-662-44335-4
Springer Heidelberg New York Dordrecht London

Library of Congress Control Number: 2014944316

LNCS Sublibrary: SL 1 – Theoretical Computer Science and General Issues

Typesetting: Camera-ready by author, data conversion by Scientific Publishing Services, Chennai, India

Printed on acid-free paper

Springer is part of Springer Science+Business Media (www.springer.com)

Preface

EvoMUSART 2014—the 3rd International Conference and the 12th European event on Biologically Inspired Music, Sound, Art and Design—took place during April 23–25, 2014 in Granada, Spain. It brought together researchers who use biologically inspired computer techniques for artistic, aesthetic, and design purposes. Researchers presented their latest work in the intersection of the fields of computer science, evolutionary systems, art, and aesthetics. As always, the atmosphere was fun, friendly, and constructive.

EvoMUSART has grown steadily since its first edition in 2003 in Essex, UK, when it was one of the Applications of Evolutionary Computing workshops. Since 2012 it has been a full conference as part of the evo* co-located events.

In 2014, for the first time, the evo* co-located events have published their proceedings as post-conference proceedings. This allows authors to revise their papers in the light of discussions that occured during the conference, and we believe it is a useful addition to the process.

EvoMUSART 2014 received 30 submissions. The peer-review process was rigorous and double-blind. The international Programme Committee, listed below, was composed of 73 members from 23 countries. EvoMUSART continued to provide useful feedback to authors: among the papers sent for full review, there were on average 3.33 reviews per paper. It also continued to ensure quality by keeping acceptance rates low: 8 papers were accepted for oral presentation (26.7% acceptance rate), and 3 for poster presentation (36.7% acceptance rate for talks and posters combined).

This volume of proceedings collects the accepted papers, which cover a wide range of topics and application areas. In particular, we emphasise that, in accordance with evoMUSART's call for papers, papers dealing with "biologically inspired computer techniques" (not just evolutionary computation) are regarded by evoMUSART as on-topic. All the papers described below were presented as talks, except where noted as "poster presentation".

The two Best Paper Award nominees were in the domain of interaction. Eisenmann et al. improved on their previous evoMUSART work, allowing the user to specify particular parts of the evolving designs which should be regarded as fixed, and using sensitivity analysis to perform the necessary "backward mapping" from parts of the phenotype to the genotype. It is a very interesting method which might be of use in many other interactive evolutionary art and design systems.

Machado et al. proposed a new system allowing users to interactively specify their goals (fitness function components) for a non-interactive generative art system, along the way learning about what types of goals are usable to artists. This excellent work was the eventual Best Paper Award winner.

A complex and interesting genotype-phenotype mapping, employed in an interactive museum exhibit, was used as the jumping-off point by McCormack for a discussion of search space desiderata, including both variety and utility. The search space and the genotype-phenotype mapping were also the focus of Nicolau and Costelloe (poster presentation), who showed that a genome of 64 bits, with a carefully-designed mapping, could provide a very rich and varied space of images to explore.

As in recent years the evoMUSART community has made real progress by focusing on computational aesthetics. Carballal et al. and Bishop et al. each produced new sets of image features which perform well in classification experiments and may prove useful in future non-interactive evolutionary art systems, and similar scenarios. Meanwhile Castro et al. presented a system for automated author identification in images. They used experiments with human users to ground their findings in human perception, an experimental regime which can be difficult but is scientifically rewarding.

Greenfield (poster presentation) also approached the automated evolution of images but with a novel angle, rewarding individuals whose potential offspring exhibit high diversity.

The world of sound and music was represented this year by two papers. Johnson et al. presented interactive, gesture-controlled harmonization based on the corpus of J.S. Bach chorales. Stoll (poster presentation) also described a corpus-based system, in which a corpus of sampled sounds are processed by creative sound treatments, represented in the SuperCollider language, and evolved using a genetic algorithm.

Finally, Byrne et al. demonstrated a new system for optimizing 3D designs for aircraft, showing the power of evolutionary design to work with existing tools, such as the pre-existing fluid dynamics system used here to provide measures of fitness.

We thank all authors for submitting their work, including those whose work was not accepted for presentation. As always, the standard of submissions was high, and good papers had to be rejected.

The work of reviewing is done voluntarily and generally without official recognition from the institutions where reviewers are employed. Nevertheless, good reviewing is essential to a healthy conference. Therefore we particularly thank the members of the Program Committee for their hard work and professionalism in providing constructive and fair reviews.

EvoMUSART 2014 was part of the evo* 2014 event, which included 4 additional conferences: euroGP 2014, evoCOP 2014, evoBIO 2014, and evoApplications 2014. Many people helped to make this event a success.

We thank the University of Granada, especially Dr José Luis Verdegay Galdeano, University CTO and Dr Joaquín Fernández Valdivia, ETSIIT director. We thank the local organizing team of Juan Julián Merelo Guervós, Victor M. Rivas Santos, Pedro A. Castillo Valdivieso, María Isabel García Arenas, Antonio M. Mora García, Pablo García-Sánchez, Antonio Fernández Ares, Javier Asensio and with the assistance of volunteers Antonio Andrés Espinosa

Serrano, Pilar Andrés Maldonado, Fernando García Lopera, Luis Reyes González, Manuel Santiago Vargas Plata, Fernando Pérez Bueno, Noelia Corredera Cruz, Ana Pérez Ruiz de Adana, Anggella Fortunato, Jose Andrés Coba Requena, Daniel Miguel Parejo Muoz, and José Albert Cruz Almaguer.

We thank Marc Schoenauer, Inria Saclay – Île-de-France for continued assistance in providing MyReview conference management system. We thank Mauro Castelli, ISEGI, Universidade Nova de Lisboa, Portugal and Pablo García Sánchez, University of Granada, Spain for evo* publicity. We thank Kevin Sim, Institute for Informatics & Digital Information, Edinburgh Napier University for website support and logo design. We also thank the program chairs of all evo* events.

Finally and in particular we thank Jennifer Willies and the Institute for Informatics & Digital Information at Edinburgh Napier University, UK for evo* coordination and financial administration

April 2014   Juan Romero
                                                   James McDermott
                                                     João Correia

Organization

EvoMUSART 2014 was part of evo* 2014, Europe's premier co-located events in the field of evolutionary computing, which also included the conferences euroGP 2014, evoCOP 2014, evoBIO 2014 and evoApplications 2014.

Organizing Committee

Conference Chairs

Juan Romero	Universidade da Coruña, Spain
James McDermott	University College Dublin, Ireland

Publication Chair

João Correia	University of Coimbra, Portugal

Program Committee

Adrian Carballal	University of A Coruña, Spain
Alain Lioret	Paris 8 University, France
Alan Dorin	Monash University, Australia
Alejandro Pazos	University of A Coruna, Spain
Alice Eldridge	Monash University, Australia
Amilcar Cardoso	University of Coimbra, Portugal
Amy K. Hoover	University of Central Florida, USA
Andrew Brown	Griffith University, Australia
Andrew Gildfind	Google, Inc., Australia
Andrew Horner	University of Science & Technology, Hong Kong
Anna Ursyn	University of Northern Colorado, USA
Antonino Santos	University of A Coruna, Spain
Antonios Liapis	IT University of Copenhagen, Denmark
Antonio Mora	Granada University, Spain
Arne Eigenfeldt	Simon Fraser University, Canada
Artemis Sanchez Moroni	Renato Archer Research Center, Brazil
Benjamin Schroeder	Ohio State University, USA
Benjamin Smith	Indianapolis University, Purdue University, Indianapolis, USA
Bill Manaris	College of Charleston, USA
Brian Ross	Brock University, Canada
Carlos Grilo	Instituto Politécnico de Leiria, Portugal

Christian Jacob	University of Calgary, Canada
Colin Johnson	University of Kent, UK
Dan Ashlock	University of Guelph, Canada
Dan Costelloe	Independent Researcher (Solace One Ltd), Ireland
Dan Ventura	Brigham Young University, USA
Daniel Bisig	University of Zurich, Switzerland
Daniel Jones	Goldsmiths College, University of London, UK
Daniel Silva	University of Coimbra, Portugal
Douglas Repetto	Columbia University, USA
Eduardo Miranda	University of Plymouth, UK
Eelco den Heijer	Vrije Universiteit Amsterdam, The Netherlands
Eleonora Bilotta	University of Calabria, Italy
Francois Pachet	Sony CSL Paris, France
Gary Greenfield	University of Richmond, USA
Gary Nelson	Oerlin College, USA
Hans Dehlinger	Independent Artist, Germany
Hernán Kerlleñevich	National University of Quilmes, Argentina
J.E. Rowe	University of Birmingham, UK
James McDermott	University College Dublin, Ireland
Jane Prophet	Independent Artist, UK
Juan Romero	University of A Coruña, Spain
John Collomosse	University of Surrey, UK
Jon McCormack	Monash University, Australia
Jonathan Byrne	University College Dublin, Ireland
Jonathan Eisenmann	Ohio State University, USA
José Fornari	NICS/Unicamp, Brazil
Kate Reed	Imperial College, UK
Marcelo Freitas Caetano	IRCAM, France
Marcos Nadal	University of Illes Balears, Spain
Matthew Lewis	Ohio State University, USA
Mauro Annunziato	Plancton Art Studio, Italy
Maximos Kaliakatsos Papakostas	University of Patras, Greece
Michael O'Neill	University College Dublin, Ireland
Nicolas Monmarché	University of Tours, France
Pablo Gervás	Universidad Complutense de Madrid, Spain
Palle Dahlstedt	Göteborg University, Sweden
Patrick Janssen	National University of Singapore, Singapore
Paulo Urbano	Universidade de Lisboa, Portugal
Pedro Abreu	University of Coimbra, Portugal
Pedro Cruz	University of Coimbra, Portugal
Penousal Machado	University of Coimbra, Portugal

Table of Contents

Probabilistic Decision Making for Interactive Evolution with Sensitivity
Analysis . . . ./.   1
    Jonathan Eisenmann, Matthew Lewis, and Rick Parent

An Interface for Fitness Function Design   13
    Penousal Machado, Tiago Martins, Hugo Amaro,
    and Pedro H. Abreu

Balancing Act: Variation and Utility in Evolutionary Art   26
    Jon McCormack

Size Does Not Matter: Evolving Parameters for a Cayley Graph
Visualiser Using 64 Bits   38
    Miguel Nicolau and Dan Costelloe

A Complexity Approach for Identifying Aesthetic Composite
Landscapes.   50
    Adrian Carballal, Rebeca Perez, Antonino Santos, and Luz Castro

Feature Construction Using Genetic Programming for Classification
of Images by Aesthetic Value   62
    Andrew Bishop, Vic Ciesielski, and Karen Trist

Authorship and Aesthetics Experiments: Comparison of Results
between Human and Computational Systems   74
    Luz Castro, Rebeca Perez, Antonino Santos, and Adrian Carballal

An Indirect Fitness Scheme for Automated Evolution of Aesthetic
Images   85
    Gary Greenfield

A Novelty Search and Power-Law-Based Genetic Algorithm
for Exploring Harmonic Spaces in J.S. Bach Chorales   95
    Bill Manaris, David Johnson, and Yiorgos Vassilandonakis

Genomic: Evolving Sound Treatments Using Genetic Algorithms   107
  Thomas M. Stoll

Evolving an Aircraft Using a Parametric Design System   119
  *Jonathan Byrne, Philip Cardiff, Anthony Brabazon,
  and Michael O'Neill*

Author Index   131

Probabilistic Decision Making for Interactive Evolution with Sensitivity Analysis

Jonathan Eisenmann[1,2], Matthew Lewis[2], and Rick Parent[1]

[1] Department of Computer Science and Engineering
[2] The Advanced Computing Center for the Arts and Design (ACCAD),
The Ohio State University, Columbus, OH 43210, USA

Abstract. Recent research in the area of evolutionary algorithms and interactive design tools for ideation has investigated how sensitivity analysis can be used to enable region-of-interest selection on design candidates. Even though it provides more precise control over the evolutionary search to the designer, the existing methodology for this enhancement to evolutionary algorithms does not make full use of the information provided by sensitivity analysis and may lead to premature convergence. In this paper, we describe the shortcomings of previous research on this topic and introduce an approach that mitigates the problem of early convergence. A discussion of the trade-offs of different approaches to sensitivity analysis is provided as well as a demonstration of this new technique on a parametric model built for character design ideation.

Keywords: interactive evolution, sensitivity analysis, probabilistic genetic operators.

1 Introduction

For subjective tasks, interactive evolutionary algorithms can provide a robust and intuitive way to traverse large, high-dimensional design spaces. Ideation tools based on evolutionary algorithms seek to aid human designers as they form, and possibly re-form, their design goals with continued exposure to ideas generated with the algorithm. One widely recognized problem with these design tools is designer fatigue. The algorithm can generate candidate solutions endlessly, but the human-in-the-loop has limited patience, attention, and energy. The available search time is bound by these human limitations and must be well spent.

Previous research on interactive evolution with region-of-interest selection has provided a potential path forward for addressing the human fatigue bottleneck [3,20]. These systems seek to maximize the synergy between algorithmic computation and human subjective reasoning by extracting more information from the

J. Romero et al. (Eds.): EvoMUSART 2014, LNCS 8601, pp. 1–12, 2014.

user's selections at a fine-grain level, to discover important parts of design candidates. Using this additional information, these systems lock down certain model parameters, effectively culling the search space and speeding up convergence.

Any time part of the search space is excluded, care must be taken to ensure that the culling is not too aggressive, otherwise premature convergence may occur. In this paper we take a closer look at ways in which the solution put forth in our previous work in this area can lead to such a scenario, and then we describe a new approach which avoids aggressive culling of the space, while still providing steering for the evolutionary algorithm.

2   Related Work

Soon after Dawkins's pioneering work with biomorphs[2], the work of Sims[18] and Todd & Latham[22] laid the foundation for the coming growth of interactive evolution as a research area. For an exhaustive overview of interactive evolutionary design research, we refer the reader to surveys by Lewis[10], Semet[15], and Takagi[21]. In the remainder of this section, we will briefly survey sensitivity analysis and how it has been used in combination with evolutionary algorithms, and then proceed to discuss related work dealing with region-of-interest selection in evolutionary systems.

Sensitivity analysis is a statistical tool that samples a given model to discover the sensitivities of the model inputs. Sensitivity analysis is commonly applied in computational modeling in order to provide a standard measure of the model's reliability [14]. It can identify the influence of individual inputs (first-order effects) as well as interactions between inputs (epistasis). Finding an inverse mapping from the selected component of the phenotype to the genes in the genotype responsible for the qualities of that component is the most challenging problem in building an evolutionary system that allows for region-of-interest selection. Our previous paper on partial selection with interactive evolution utilizes sensitivity analysis to address this mapping problem in a model-free way [3]. Sensitivity analysis is just one approach that is used to tackle high-dimensional design problems with black-box functions. A discussion of sensitivity analysis and other approaches to these types of problems can be found in the survey by Shan and Wang [16].

In the area of visual parametric modeling, Erhan, et al. [4] proposed a method that seeks to improve the process of visually analyzing the sensitivity of a model to changes in its parameters. In recent computer graphics literature, a furniture design framework used sensitivity analysis to identify parameters that cause physical instability so it could highlight weaknesses in the current designs [23]. In the area of multi-objective evolutionary computation Avila, et al. [1] suggested using sensitivity analysis to find a final solution from a set of candidate solutions that result from a multi-objective stochastic optimization process. Parmee, et al. [12] utilized sensitivity analysis in a non-interactive way to adjust constraint maps whose function it is to unite separate GA optimizations in a multi-objective framework near the end of the exploration phase. The objectives analyzed for sensitivity in his framework have explicit fitness functions.

Recent work in the area of region-of-interest selection for exploratory interfaces includes an interface that utilizes fuzzy correspondence based on selected parts to aid users in browsing collections of 3D models [8]. An evolutionary design example of partial selection (and modification) consists of a fashion design interface where users have access to directly manipulate components of candidate solutions using a pop-up menu. The modifications made to phenotype parts in the interface correspond directly to genotype changes [9]. Takagi and Kishi [20] have experimented with trait selection (called "online knowledge embedding") for a face photo montage application. Users of this system can lock down any piece of the montage, essentially reducing the dimensionality of the available search space and quickening convergence. The mapping from gene to trait in this system is one-to-one, so finding the inverse mapping from trait to gene in this case is not difficult. Building on this work, our previous system allows for models with interactions between genes, selection of arbitrary regions-of-interest within the phenotype, and complex relationships between genes and traits in the model [3]. However, depending on the parametric model in use, this approach may lead to premature convergence, as discussed below.

3 Method

Our previous method relies on a binary classification of model parameters as either sensitive or insensitive. This binary classification comes as a result of the typical interpretation of the elementary effects method of sensitivity analysis (see below for more details on elementary effects). While efficient in its simplicity, this approach leads to a loss of valuable sensitivity information and can result in a too aggressive culling of the search space. Depending on the nature of the relationship between the model parameters in question and other model parameters, this approach may lead to early convergence when genes are locked down prematurely because they were classified as sensitive by elementary effects.

In the following sections, we will describe two approaches to sensitivity analysis and detail how each can be utilized in a system similar to that of our previous work, but with probabilistic decision making in the genetic operators of the evolutionary algorithm. This new approach mitigates the problem of early convergence while still maintaining the interactive evolutionary algorithmic steering provided by region-of-interest selection and sensitivity analysis.

3.1 Sensitivity Analysis for Interactive Design with Parametric Models

Our goal for sensitivity analysis in this system is to ascribe reliable sensitivity measures to each input parameter of a model. The analysis consists of three stages: sampling model inputs, model evaluation, and analysis of model outputs. In general, approaches to sensitivity analysis focus on the first and last step as the model evaluation depends heavily on the parametric model being analyzed.

In the methods described below, the model evaluation process is completely parallelizable because each model evaluation is independent, even though the individual samples are not. Computation time can be saved by distributing model evaluations to separate processes or machines. In the following subsections, we will describe two approaches to sensitivity analysis that can be used with interactive evolution and at the end of this section we will discuss the trade-offs between the two methods.

Elementary Effects. Elementary effects is a screening method used primarily to determine whether or not each parameter is sensitive. It works by measuring the gradient between adjacent sampled locations in the parametric space to divide the parameters into three groups: parameters that have no effect, those that have strong linear effects, and parameters with either non-linear effects or interactions with other parameters. The particular approach we use for elementary effects is the Morris Method.

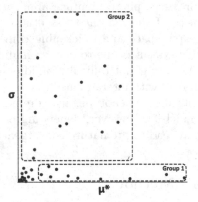

Fig. 1. Elementary Effects Results

After generating the samples $\mathbf{x}$ by taking N random walks through input space, changing one parameter at a time[1], the samples are evaluated using the parametric model $f(\mathbf{x})$, and the outputs $\mathbf{y}$ are analyzed for classification into one of the three aforementioned categories using the following steps. First the elementary effects, as defined by Morris, are computed for each of the g parameters:

$$\mathbf{ee_i} = \frac{[f(x_1, ..., x_{i-1}, x_i + \Delta, x_{i+1}, ..., x_g) - f(\mathbf{x})]}{\Delta}. \tag{1}$$

In our system, changes in the model output are measured as the sum of distances between the corresponding points in the resulting vertices of the model output[2]. Next, the elementary effects $\mathbf{ee_i}$ for each parameter i are summarized using μ_i^* and σ_i

$$\mu_i^* = 1/g * \sum_{j=1}^{N} |ee_{i_j}| \qquad (2) \qquad\qquad \sigma_i = stddev(\mathbf{ee_i}) \qquad (3)$$

Finally, $\boldsymbol{\mu^*}$ and $\boldsymbol{\sigma}$ are typically plotted as shown in figure 1. Parameters near the origin are considered to be insensitive. Parameters found along the X axis (Group 1) demonstrate strong linear effects and are considered sensitive. Parameters found in the rest of the graph (Group 2) have high standard deviation

---

[1] Refer to our previous paper [3] or the original paper by Morris [11] for the details of generating Morris samples.

[2] Other distance metrics may make more sense for a given design domain, and as long as the metric yields a one-dimensional measurement, it can be used here instead of the point cloud distance metric.

and are considered to either exhibit non-linear effects or interactions with other parameters (epistasis). Our system runs with parameter settings of $N = 20$ random walks and $L = 4$ grid levels. We use K-means to cluster the points with the aim of identifying the cluster nearest the origin and classifying the points in that cluster as insensitive. In practice, we have found that generating $K = max(3, g/3)$ clusters of points provides sufficient granularity to identify the origin cluster.

Our previous work classifies genes in a binary way as sensitive (1) or insensitive (0), effectively throwing away the rest of the information embedded in the scatter plot. In this research, we use the following heuristic to estimate total gene sensitivity S_{T_i} for genes with scatter plot points $i = 1...q$ not in the origin cluster

$$S_{all} = \sum_{i=1}^{q} \sqrt{\mu_i^{*2} + \sigma_i^2} \qquad (4) \qquad\qquad S_{T_i} \approx \frac{\sqrt{\mu_i^{*2} + \sigma_i^2}}{S_{all}} \qquad (5)$$

Given the limitations of the Morris method, this heuristic is not a precise measure of total sensitivity and correct ranking of parameters is not guaranteed. However, in practice, it is accurate enough to inform our probabilistic genetic operators and steer the evolutionary search in an intuitive way. Because of the computational advantage provided by the adjacency of the random walk samples, the number of model evaluations required for the Morris method scales linearly with the number of parameters in the model. While elementary effects methods are quick to compute, this analysis is not as comprehensive or as accurate as the analysis provided by a variance-based method.

Variance-Based Analysis. Variance-based sensitivity analysis refers to a set of methods that seek to ascribe variance in the model to each parameter. Typical measurements include first-order effects (variance attributed to one parameter only) and total sensitivity indices (total variance attributed to one parameter, including the part of the variance caused by interactions with other parameters). We have chosen to explore using the Sobol method of sensitivity analysis[3] which has the convenient property that the sum of the total sensitivity indices for all model inputs is equal to one. According to Sobol, the decomposition of total model variance by the parameters and their interactions can be expressed as

$$D(f) = \sum_i D_i + \sum_{i<j} D_{ij} + \sum_{i<j<k} D_{ijk} + D_{12...g} \qquad (6)$$

where $D(f)$ is the total variance of the parametric model f, D_i is the first-order variance attributed to the ith parameter, D_{ij} is the variance attributed to the interaction between parameters i and j, and $D_{12...g}$ contains all variance

---

[3] For details on generating Sobol sampling sequences, see the paper by Joe and Kuo [7]. For more details on the Sobol analysis method, we refer the reader to the original paper by Sobol [19].

attributable to third-order effects and higher, up to g parameters. The model outputs for Sobol analysis can be evaluated using either first order effects (equation 7) or total gene sensitivities (equation 8):

$$S_i = \frac{D_i}{D} \qquad (7) \qquad\qquad S_{T_i} = 1 - \frac{D_{\sim i}}{D} \qquad (8)$$

where D is the total model variance, D_i is the variance due to parameter i, and $D_{\sim i}$ is the variance due to all parameters but i. In this research, S_{T_i} is the more useful sensitivity measure because we are interested in the overall effect of a gene on the model output.

Practical Considerations. Now that we have described two popular approaches to sensitivity analysis, let us consider the practical trade-offs of using each method. In terms of the number of model evaluations N, Sobol scales linearly with the number of model parameters (or genes). However, in practice, the Sobol method requires a large number of model evaluations per parameter in order for the sum-to-one property to hold. For example, the Sobol method required $N = 600$ for the simple revolved surface model shown in the figures below. If N is too small, negative total sensitivity indices can result. In order to avoid negative sensitivity measures, Sobol analysis must be run for a particular parametric model with varying numbers of iterations until the minimum number of samples that reliably generates a satisfactory set of non-negative sensitivities is found.

In *interactive* evolutionary design, maintaining interactive rates is critical for maintaining the continuity of the designer's train of thought. In order to attain interactive rates, certain sacrifices in accuracy may need to be made, depending on the computational cost of evaluating the parametric model. Our previous system generated two-dimensional graphics with negligible computational cost, so a complete Sobol analysis could have been conducted while still maintaining interactive rates. In this work, we demonstrate the utility of interactive evolution of three-dimensional polygonal parametric models which require significantly more CPU time, so we use the Morris method as a heuristic approach. In a recent report by Herman, et al. the Morris method was found to correctly identify sensitive and insensitive parameters with 300 times fewer model evaluations [6], so we feel this is a reasonable choice.

3.2   Probabilistic Decision Making for the Genetic Operators

Given the added info of floating-point sensitivity measures S_{T_i}, we can avoid binary decisions and instead use probabilities along with pseudo-random numbers to determine inheritance and local search.

Any evolutionary steering based on trait selection should ensure that the selected trait is prevalent in the subsequent generation. The degree of prevalence depends on the number of parents in the gene pool during reproduction as well as the mutation strength. At the gene level, in the absence of mutation, the prevalence $Prob_i$ of a selected-for gene i can be expressed as

$$Prob_i = S_{T_i}/(NumberOfParents - 1). \qquad (9)$$

Based on our observations and experiments with the system described here, this property holds. (See figure 2.)

```
begin
    Input: Two genotypes: parent₀ and parent₁; One integer: generationCount
    Output: One genotype: child
    copyFrom = randomInteger(0, 1);
    for  i ← 0 to numGenes − 1 do
        if  random(1) < xoverChance then
        |   copyFrom = 1 − copyFrom;
        end
        if  parent₁.xoverSensitivity[i] > parent₀.xoverSensitivity[i] and
            (parent₀.xoverSensitivity[i] < 0 or random(1) < parent₁.xoverSensitivity[i])
        then
        |       child.inheritance[i] = 1;
        end
        if  parent₀.xoverSensitivity[i] > parent₁.xoverSensitivity[i] and
            (parent₁.xoverSensitivity[i] < 0 or random(1) < parent₀.xoverSensitivity[i])
        then
        |       child.inheritance[i] = 0;
        end
        else
        |   child.inheritance[i] = copyFrom;
        end
        if  child.inheritance[i] == 1 then
        |   child.genes[i] = parent₁.genes[i];
        end
        else
        |   child.genes[i] = parent₀.genes[i];
        end
    end
end
```

Algorithm 1. Crossover Algorithm

Crossover. Using the probabilistic crossover as outlined in Algorithm 1 with additional probabilistic decision making regarding sensitivity values, we avoid overly aggressive lock-down of sensitive genes. By way of example, we have concocted a simple parametric revolved surface model with five parameters in the range $[0, 1]$: a style selector, flare width, neck thickness, width, and height. The style selector parameter in this case is an example of how premature culling of the search space due to epistasis can occur. This parameter acts as a four-way switch: values below 0.25 result in no flare, between 0.25 and 0.5 result in bottom-only flare, between 0.5 and 0.75 result in top and bottom flare, and finally values above 0.75 result in top-only flare.

In figure 2, the simple case of two parent, crossover-only reproduction is shown. Parent B has an emphasis selection of the vertices at its base (indicated by the highlighted vertices). The genes to which this region is sensitive will have positive sensitivity indices above 0.0, and all the rest of the genes will have sensitivities of 0.0. The offspring population on the left demonstrates our previous method, which can be seen to exhibit overly aggressive lock-down of the sensitive genes (flare width, style selector, and width) because their sensitivities are set to 1.0. On the right, our new method exhibits a more reasonable biased crossover behavior resulting from algorithm 1 and gene sensitivities for flare width, style selector, and width of 21%, 56%, and 23% respectively.

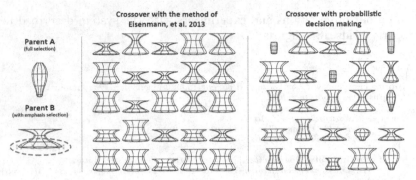

Fig. 2. Crossover-only reproduction comparsion (crossover probability = 25%)

```
begin
    Input: Three genotypes: child, parent₀, parent₁; One integer: generation
    Output: One genotype: mutatedChild
    for i ← 0 to numGenes − 1 do
        noiz = udn((i + generation) * 1.5 + 231,
                   (parent₀.id + parent₁.id) * 1.4 + 895,
                   child.id * 1.6 + 387);
        if noiz < mutationChance then
            if child.inheritanceᵢ == 0 then
            |    currentParent = parent₀;
            end
            else
            |    currentParent = parent₁;
            end
            if currentParent.mutationSensitivityᵢ < mutationChance then
                mutatedChild.genesᵢ = child.genesᵢ;
                mutation = mutationAmount * (noiz * 2 − 1);
                mutatedChild.genesᵢ+ = mutation;
                mutatedChild.genesᵢ = clamp(mutatedChild.genesᵢ, 0, 1);
            end
        end
    end
end
```

Algorithm 2. Mutation Algorithm

Mutation. Similarly, using this probabilistic decision making in mutation yields more diverse results. Using the same model and region selection with a different parent in figure 3, the previous method yields a less diverse population by locking down the genes that control flare width, style selector, and width, while the method presented here yields more reasonable mutation results based on the sensitivity indices of 18%, 55%, and 27% respectively. Also, we have found uniformly distributed[4] Perlin noise [13] to be useful in generating pseudo-random numbers for our mutation operator as it provides predictable and smoothly controllable randomness, which is particularly useful when we allow the designer to interactively adjust mutation strength with a slider and immediately see results in the population. Using noise for this minimizes the "pops" or dramatic phenotypic changes that might happen with a standard random number generator.

---

[4] $udn(\mathbf{x}) = smoothstep(0.25, 0.75, noise(\mathbf{x}))$

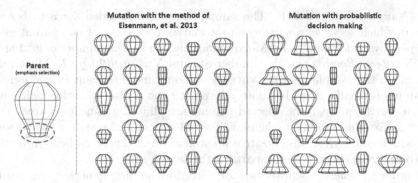

Fig. 3. Mutation-only reproduction comparison (mutation probability = 100% and mutation amount = 0.4)

In addition to standard full candidate selection, there are three types of sensitivity-enabled region selection that could prove to be useful: emphasis, partial, and reject selection. Emphasis selection could be used when a designer is interested in the whole candidate, but wishes to emphasize a certain trait. It works, similarly to our previous method by assigning positive sensitivity values to sensitive genes and zeros to other genes. In this way, our crossover algorithm treats the insensitive genes as normal, equal members of the gene pool, while the sensitive genes get probabilistic preference. Partial selection may prove useful when the designer is interested only in part of the candidate and not in the other parts. It works similarly to emphasis selection except the insensitive genes are assigned values of -1.0, so they will never by chosen by crossover. Finally reject selection can be used by the designer to select a "bad" trait from an interesting candidate and exclude that trait from the subsequent population. Here the sensitive gene values are negated and the insensitive genes are set to zero.

It is important to note that our system maintains no memory of sensitivity values beyond one generation other than implicit memory of the gene pool. It could be counterproductive for the selected traits from one generation to directly influence the reproduction process several generations later because the designer may change his mind about what is fit.

3.3 Sampling Modifications

The sensitivity analysis methods outlined above sample the parametric search space globally. In order to provide sensitivity analysis that is relevant to the crossover and mutation operators, it is necessary to make some changes to the sampling process. The guiding principle here is that the gene sensitivity being measured should have a direct correlation to the operation to be performed on that gene.

For crossover, this means the system should measure how sensitive a particular gene is to replacement by other genes from the set of selected parents (not a random value from the global parametric space). Therefore we generate global samples with values that range from 0 to 1, then multiply each gene sample value by the number of candidates in the gene pool to get values from

0 to ($NumberOfParents - 1$). The samples are then rounded down to become integers which serve as row indices to a matrix consisting of one parent genotype per row. Additionally, for Morris sampling, we set the number of grid levels $L = NumberOfParents$ and the number of runs $N = min(20, g * L)$. This modification to the sampling for crossover is not only more efficient (if the number of parents is small), it is also more relevant to the actual operation being performed. Furthermore, if the selected parents are all in the same local area of the search space, this sampling scheme will avoid a potential pitfall of global analysis, which could yield false positive identification of a gene as being sensitive, due to sensitive effects in other parts of the search space.

In order to generate sensitivities for mutation, we first generate samples between 0 and 1, then scale the samples using the mutation amount set by the designer. The samples for each gene are subsequently offset so that they straddle the current gene value of the genotype being mutated. One further modification that enables our mutation slider to maintain interactive rates is that mutation sensitivities are sampled with multiple, evenly-spaced scales and sensitivity analysis for each scale is run at the end of population reproduction. Later, when the designer is interacting with the mutation slider, the mutation sensitivities are calculated by linearly interpolating between these pre-computed sensitivities in real-time.

4   Results

Figure 4 demonstrates the difference in inheritance provided by trait selection on phenotypes generated from a parametric model created in Houdini [17] in collaboration with one of the design and animation students from our research facility. He wanted to explore visual options for the giant rock character in his thesis film. The polygonal model has 1533 vertices and 60 separate procedural operations, including body part deformations, breaking of limbs, and proportional changes in scale. Each model evaluation takes 1.1 CPU seconds and a typical time between generations with our system (using the Morris method) is about a minute. You can find a video showing population convergence over time with both methods at (http://accad.osu.edu/Projects/Evo/ProbabilisticSensitiveEvo/).

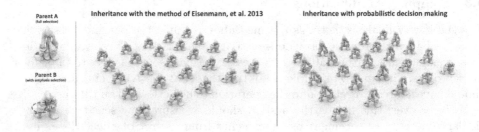

Fig. 4. Comparison of reproduction with both crossover and mutation in a character design session. Our new method is on the right.

5   Conclusion

In summary, we have introduced and demonstrated new probabilistic decision making algorithms for both the crossover and mutation operators. These algorithms alleviate the problem of premature convergence found in our previous system while still maintaining the steering that sensitivity analysis can provide to an interactive evolutionary design system. Furthermore, we have introduced a novel crossover sampling strategy that is more relevant to the operation being measured for sensitivity.

Acknowledgments. Many thanks to Tom Heban for making his character model available for this research. We would like to express out gratitude to J.D. Herman for posting his useful SALib to GitHub [5]. The Houdini procedural graphics software has proven to be an enjoyable development environment for creating and manipulating complex parametric models [17]. Thanks are also due to the Advanced Computing Center for the Arts and Design (ACCAD) for providing a truly collaborative and interdisciplinary work environment.

References

1. Avila, S.L., Lisboa, A.C., Krahenbuhl, L., Carpes, W.P., Vasconcelos, J.A., Saldanha, R.R., Takahashi, R.H.C.: Sensitivity analysis applied to decision making in multiobjective evolutionary optimization. IEEE Transactions on Magnetics 42(4), 1103–1106 (2006), http://dx.doi.org/10.1109/tmag.2006.871447
2. Dawkins, R.: The Blind Watchmaker: Why the Evidence of Evolution Reveals a Universe Without Design. Norton (1986), http://books.google.com/books?id=sPpaZnZMDGOC
3. Eisenmann, J., Lewis, M., Parent, R.: Inverse Mapping with Sensitivity Analysis for Partial Selection in Interactive Evolution. In: Machado, P., McDermott, J., Carballal, A. (eds.) EvoMUSART 2013. LNCS, vol. 7834, pp. 72–84. Springer, Heidelberg (2013)
4. Erhan, H., Woodbury, R., Salmasi, N.H.: Visual sensitivity analysis of parametric design models: improving agility in design. Master's thesis, School of Interactive Arts and Technology - Simon Fraser University (2009)
5. Herman, J.D.: SALib (October 2013), https://github.com/jdherman/SALib
6. Herman, J.D., Kollat, J.B., Reed, P.M., Wagener, T.: Technical note: Method of Morris effectively reduces the computational demands of global sensitivity analysis for distributed watershed models. Hydrology and Earth System Sciences Discussions 10(4), 4275–4299 (2013), http://dx.doi.org/10.5194/hessd-10-4275-2013
7. Joe, S., Kuo, F.Y.: Constructing Sobol Sequences with Better Two-Dimensional Projections. SIAM J. Sci. Comput. 30(5), 2635–2654 (2008), http://dx.doi.org/10.1137/070709359
8. Kim, V.G., Li, W., Mitra, N.J., DiVerdi, S., Funkhouser, T.: Exploring collections of 3D models using fuzzy correspondences. ACM Trans. Graph. 31(4) (July 2012), http://dx.doi.org/10.1145/2185520.2185550

12   J. Eisenmann, M. Lewis, and R. Parent

9. Lee, J.H., Kim, H.S., Cho, S.B.: Accelerating evolution by direct manipulation for interactive fashion design. In: Proceedings Fourth International Conference on Computational Intelligence and Multimedia Applications, ICCIMA 2001, pp. 343–347. IEEE (2001), http://dx.doi.org/10.1109/iccima.2001.970491
10. Lewis, M.: Evolutionary Visual Art and Design. In: Romero, J., Machado, P. (eds.) The Art of Artificial Evolution: A Handbook on Evolutionary Art and Music, pp. 3–37. Springer, Heidelberg (2007)
11. Morris, M.D.: Factorial Sampling Plans for Preliminary Computational Experiments. Technometrics 33(2), 161–174 (1991), http://dx.doi.org/10.2307/1269043
12. Parmee, I.C., Cvetković, D.C., Watson, A.H., Bonham, C.R.: Multiobjective Satisfaction within an Interactive Evolutionary Design Environment. Evol. Comput. 8(2), 197–222 (2000), http://dx.doi.org/10.1162/106365600568176
13. Perlin, K.: Improving noise. ACM Trans. Graph. 21(3), 681–682 (2002), http://dx.doi.org/10.1145/566570.566636
14. Saltelli, A., Chan, K.: Scott: Sensitivity analysis. J. Wiley & Sons. (2000), http://www.worldcat.org/isbn/0470743824
15. Semet, Y.: Interactive Evolutionary Computation: a survey of existing theory (2002), http://citeseerx.ist.psu.edu/viewdoc/summary?doi=10.1.1.108.7832
16. Shan, S., Wang, G.G.: Survey of modeling and optimization strategies to solve high-dimensional design problems with computationally-expensive black-box functions. Structural and Multidisciplinary Optimization 41(2), 219–241 (2010), http://dx.doi.org/10.1007/s00158-009-0420-2
17. Side Effects Software: HOUDINI FX. houdini (2013), http://www.sidefx.com
18. Sims, K.: Artificial evolution for computer graphics. In: SIGGRAPH 1991 Proceedings, vol. 25, pp. 319–328. ACM, New York (1991), http://dx.doi.org/10.1145/122718.122752
19. Sobol, I.M.: Global sensitivity indices for nonlinear mathematical models and their Monte Carlo estimates. Mathematics and Computers in Simulation 55(1-3), 271–280 (2001), http://dx.doi.org/10.1016/s0378-47540000270-6
20. Takagi, H., Kishi, K.: On-line knowledge embedding for an interactive EC-based montage system, pp. 280–283 (December 1999), http://dx.doi.org/10.1109/kes.1999.820178
21. Takagi, H.: New IEC Research and Frameworks Aspects of Soft Computing, Intelligent Robotics and Control. In: Fodor, J., Kacprzyk, J. (eds.) Aspects of Soft Computing, Intelligent Robotics and Control. SCI, vol. 241, pp. 65–76. Springer, Heidelberg (2009), http://dx.doi.org/10.1007/978-3-642-03633-0_4
22. Todd, S., Latham, W.: Evolutionary art and computers. Academic Press (1992), http://www.worldcat.org/isbn/9780124371859
23. Umetani, N., Igarashi, T., Mitra, N.J.: Guided Exploration of Physically Valid Shapes for Furniture Design. ACM Transactions on Graphics (Proceedings of SIGGRAPH 2012) 31(4) (2012)

An Interface for Fitness Function Design

Penousal Machado, Tiago Martins, Hugo Amaro, and Pedro H. Abreu

CISUC, Department of Informatics Engineering, University of Coimbra,
3030 Coimbra, Portugal
{machado,tiagofm,pha}@dei.uc.pt, hamaro@student.dei.uc.pt

Abstract. Fitness assignment is one of the biggest challenges in evolutionary art. Interactive evolutionary computation approaches put a significant burden on the user, leading to human fatigue. On the other hand, autonomous evolutionary art systems usually fail to give the users the opportunity to express and convey their artistic goals and preferences. Our approach empowers the users by allowing them to express their intentions through the design of fitness functions. We present a novel responsive interface for designing fitness function in the scope of evolutionary ant paintings. Once the evolutionary runs are concluded, further control is given to the users by allowing them to specify the rendering details of selected pieces. The analysis of the experimental results highlights how fitness function design influences the outcomes of the evolutionary runs, conveying the intentions of the user and enabling the evolution of a wide variety of images.

Keywords: Ant Paintings, Fitness Function, Autonomous Evolutionary Art.

1 Introduction

According to McCormack [13] evolutionary aesthetic search implies two main considerations: (i) The design of a generative system that creates individuals; (ii) The evaluation of the fitness of such individuals. Furthermore, there are two basic approaches to fitness evaluation: (i) Interactive Evolutionary Computation (IEC); (ii) Some form of automated fitness assignment. Although some systems use a combination of these two approaches, the majority focuses on one of them.

IEC allows the users to express their preferences and directly influence the course of evolution, allowing them, in theory, to guide it towards regions of the space that match their goals. However, this comes with a burden: the need to evaluate a vast number of individuals. In practice, more often than not, human fatigue prevents the prolific exploration of the search space. The study of automated fitness assignment may bring insights towards a better understanding of aesthetics, and while it is an effective way of fighting human fatigue. However, to some extent, the solution defeats the purpose since the users are no longer able to express their preferences. Thus, automated aesthetic fitness assignment is vital for the development of an autonomous evolutionary artist. However, it falls short when the goal is to design a creativity support tool that allows the users to express their artistic preferences and intentions. Machine learning techniques

J. Romero et al. (Eds.): EvoMUSART 2014, LNCS 8601, pp. 13–25, 2014.

have been used to capture the aesthetic preferences of users with some degree of success (see e.g. [3]). We argue that although such techniques have a role in the development of creativity support tools, the state of the art hasn't reached the level where these techniques would suffice on their own.

Machado and Pereira [12] presented a non-photorealistic rendering (NPR) algorithm inspired by ant colony approaches, where the trails of artificial ants were used to produce a rendering of an original input image. The large number of parameters controlling the behavior of the ants, and the dependencies among parameters, prevented their tuning by hand. As such, an IEC approach was adopted [12]. Instead of being forced to perform low-level changes, users become breeders of species of ants that produce results that they find valuable. The experimental results showed that human fatigue was taking its toll: only the disciplined and patient users were able to guide the algorithm towards non-trivial combinations of parameters. Most users adopted an opportunistic approach, valuing novelty over quality. Additionally, when the users started the process with a specific type of image in mind, e.g. a rendering consisting exclusively of straight lines, they failed to reach their goal.

In this paper a novel interface for the design of fitness functions is described. This frees the users from the need to perform individual assessments allowing them to express their aesthetic and artistic goals by specifying the characteristics they desire or which to avoid. While the ants paint, statistics describing their behavior are gathered, and when the painting is completed, image features are calculated. These behavioral and image features are the basis for the creation of the fitness functions. The exact meaning of each of these features and the interdependencies among them may be difficult to grasp by the common user. To tackle this problem, the interface is responsive, allowing the user to perceive the semantics associated with each feature. Once the evolutionary runs are concluded we further empower the users by letting them to select their favorite phenotypes, apply the associated genotypes to different input images, and control the details of the final rendering.

2   State of the Art

Tzafestas [22] presents a system where artificial ants pick-up and deposit food, which is represented by paint, studying the self-regulation properties of the system and complexity of the resulting images. Ramos and Almeida [18] explore the use of ant systems for pattern recognition purposes. The artificial ants successfully detect the edges of the images producing stylized renderings of the originals. The artistic potential of the approach is explored in later work [17]. Urbano [23] describes a multi-agent system based on artificial ants, presenting the first artificial ant paintings produced using a faithful biological model in [24].

Aupetit et al. [1] introduce an interactive Genetic Algorithm (GA) for the creation of ant paintings. The algorithm evolves parameters of the rules that govern the behavior of the ants. The artificial ants deposit paint on the canvas as they move, thus producing a painting. In a later study, Monmarché et al. [14]

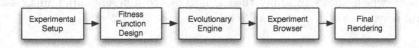

Fig. 1. The pipeline

refine this approach exploring different rendering modes. Semet et al. [21] applied ant colony simulation to produce NPRs of input images. For the same purpose, Fernandes et al. [4] use an approach akin to Ramos and Almeida [18]. Greenfield [5] presents an evolutionary approach to the production of ant paintings and explores the use of behavioral statistics of the artificial ants to automatically assign fitness. Later he adopted a multiple pheromone model where ants' movements and behaviors are influenced (attracted or repelled) by both an environmentally generated pheromone and an ant generated pheromone [6].

The use of evolutionary algorithms to create image filters and NPRs of source images has been explored by several researchers. Focusing on works where there was an artistic goal: Ross et al. [19,15] use Genetic Programming, multi-objective optimization techniques, and an empirical model of aesthetics to automatically evolve image filters; Lewis [9], evolves live-video processing filters through interactive evolution; Machado et al. [10], use GP to evolve image coloring filters from a set of examples; Yip [25] employs GAs to evolve filters that produce images that match certain features of a target image; Collomosse [2] uses image salience metrics to determine the level of detail for portions of the image, and GAs to search for painterly renderings that match the desired salience maps; Hewgill and Ross [7] use GP to evolve procedural textures for 3D objects. Schlechtweg et al. [20] adopt a, non-evolutionary, multi-agent approach for stroke-based rendering.

3   The Framework

Figure 1 describes our pipeline. The users begin by setting up the experiment establishing parameters such as: input image, population size, number of generations, number of runs, crossover and mutation rate. Then, using the responsive interface, they design a fitness function that will be used to guide evolution. Control is then passed to the evolutionary engine. Each genotype of the GA population encodes the parameters of a species of ants. These parameters determine how that ant species reacts to the input image. Each painting, i.e. each phenotype, is produced by simulating the behavior of ants of a given species while they travel across the canvas, leaving a trail of varying width and transparency. When the evolutionary runs are finished, the users select individuals that match their artistic intentions. This can be done by browsing through the populations, but it is usually more effective to consult the "summary" windows that depict the fittest individuals of a run and the fittest individuals of each generation. The chosen individuals are then passed to the final rendering interface, which allows to apply their genotypes to different input images and control several aspects of the final rendering.

3.1 Ants' Simulation

Our ants live on a 2D environment initialized with the input image and they paint on a painting canvas that is initially empty (i.e., black). The painting canvas is used exclusively for depositing ink. The luminance of an area of the environment is the available energy at that point. During simulation, ants gain energy traveling through bright areas, and this energy is removed from the environment. If the energy of an ant is below a given threshold it dies, if it is above a given threshold it generates offspring. The ants' movement is determined by how they react to light. Each ant has 10 sensory vectors, each with a given direction and length. These sensory organs return the luminance value of the area where each vector ends. To update the position of an ant one performs a weighted sum, calculating the sum of the sensory vectors divided by their norms, multiplied by the luminance of their end point and by the weight the ant gives to each sensor. The result of this operation is multiplied by a scaling factor that represents the ant's base speed. Subsequently, to represent inaccuracy of movement and sensory organs, the direction is perturbed by the addition of Perlin [16] noise to its angle. Each ant has a position, color, deposit transparency and energy; all the remaining parameters are shared by the entire species. Color is determined at birth, each ant assumes the color of the area of the environment where it was born, and does not change throughout its life. Thus, the ants may carry this color to areas of the canvas that possess different colors in the original image. A detailed description of the ants' simulation can be found in [12]. The video cdv.dei.uc.pt/2014/sim.mov depicts this simulation showing the environment and painting canvas.

3.2 Extracted Features

During the simulation of each ant species, i.e. the rendering of each phenotype, a series of behavioral statistics is collected, namely: $avg(ants)$ – average number of living ants; $deposited_{ink}$ – total amount of "ink" deposited by the ants; $coverage$ – percentage of the environment visited by the ants; $avg(distance)$ – average euclidean distance between the position where the ant was born and the one where it died; $avg(trail), std(trail)$ – average trail length and the standard deviation of the trail lengths; $avg(life), std(life)$ – average life span of the ants and its standard deviation; $avg(avg(width)), std(avg(width))$ – determined by calculating for each trail the average width, and then the average width of all trails, $avg(avg(width))$, and the standard deviation of the averages, $std(avg(width))$; $avg(std(width)), std(std(width))$ – determined by calculating for each trail the standard deviation of its width, then their average, $avg(std(width))$, and their standard deviation $std(std(width))$; $avg(avg(av)), std(avg(av)), avg(std(av)), std(std(av))$ which are analogous to the features regarding trail width, but pertaining to the angular velocity of the ants;

Table 1. Parameters encoded by the genotype

Name	#	Comments
$gain$	1	scaling for energy gains
$decay$	1	scaling for energy decay
$cons_{rate}$	1	scaling for size of circles drawn on the environment
$cons_{trans}$	1	transparency of circles drawn on the environment
$deposit_{rate}$	1	scaling for size of circles drawn on the painting canvas
$deposit_{transp}$	1	base transparency of circles drawn on the painting canvas
$dtransp_{min}$	1	limits for perturbation of deposit transparency when
$dtransp_{max}$	1	offsprings are generated
$initial_{energy}$	1	initial energy of the starting ants
$death_{threshold}$	1	death energy threshold
$birth_{threshold}$	1	generate offspring energy threshold
$descvel_{min}$	1	limits for perturbation of angular velocity when
$descvel_{max}$	1	offsprings are generated
vel	1	base speed of the ants
$noise_{min}$	1	limits for the perlin noise
$noise_{max}$	1	generator function
$initial_{positions}$	$2*n$	initial coordinates of the n ants placed on the canvas
$sensory_{vectors}$	$2*m$	direction and length of the m sensory vectors
$sensory_{weights}$	m	weights of the m sensory vectors

When the simulation of each ant species ends, the following image features are collected: *complexity* – the image produced by the ants, I, is encoded in *jpeg* format, and its complexity estimated using the following formula: $complexity(I) = rmse(I, jpeg(I)) \times \frac{s(jpeg(I))}{s(I)}$, where $rmse$ stands for the root mean square error, $jpeg(I)$ is the image resulting from the *jpeg* compression of I, and s is the file size function; $fract_{dim}, lac$ – fractal dimension of the ant painting estimated by the box-counting method and its λ lacunarity value estimated by the sliding box method [8], respectively; *similarity* – similarity between the ant painting and the original image estimated as follows: $similarity = \frac{1}{1+rmse(I,O)}$, where I is the ant painting and O is the original image.

3.3 Evolutionary Engine

A GA is used to evolve the ant species' parameters. The genotypes are tuples of floating point numbers which encode the parameters of the ant species. Table 1 presents an overview of the encoded parameters. We use a two point crossover operator for recombination purposes and a Gaussian mutation operator. We employ tournament selection and an elitist strategy, the highest ranked individual proceeds – unchanged – to the next population.

4   The Anatomy of a Fitness Function

The fitness functions assume the form of a weighted sum. For each feature the user may indicate a weight, w_i, and the intention to minimize, maximize or

make the feature match a target value. Specifying a target value implies that
the fitness component associated with that feature is:

$$f_i = \frac{1}{1 + |target_{value_i} - feature_{value_i}|}$$

When the goal is to maximize a given feature, we use:

$$f_i = abs\left(\frac{feature_i}{offlinemax(feature_i)}\right),$$

where *offlinemax* returns the maximum possible value found for that feature.
This value can be established analytically for certain features, e.g. fractal dimension never exceeds 2, and it was found empirically for the remaining ones.
To prevent the evolutionary algorithm from focusing exclusively on a given feature we employ a logarithmic scale so that the evolutionary advantage decreases
as the feature value becomes higher, promoting the discovery of individuals that
use all features employed in the fitness function. This is accomplished using:
$f_i' = log(1 + f_i)$. For minimization we use the same formulas as for maximization, but f_i' returns a negative value: $f_i' = -log(1 + f_i)$. Considering all of the
above the fitness functions are given by: $\sum_{i=1}^{features} w_i \times f_i'$, where w_i is a value
in the $[-1, 1]$ interval.

5   Fitness Function Design Interface

The interface is composed of a set of responsive "icons", one for each of the features. The vertical slider on the right of each icon specifies the weight associated
with each feature. Pressing the rightmost button beneath each icon indicates
maximization of the corresponding feature, while pressing the leftmost button
indicates minimization. Specifying a target value for a feature is accomplished
using the plus and minus buttons. for most user indicating a specific value for
something as the *complexity* of an image would be meaningless. To circumvent
this problem all values are specified in the $[0, 1]$ interval and then mapped to
$[offlinemin(feature_i), offlinemax(feature_i)]$. Thus, specifying a target value of,
e.g., 0.8 for a given feature and a positive weight indicates the wish to reach a
value close to its maximum; conversely, indicating a value of 0.2 indicates the
wish to reach a value close to its minimum. Specifying a negative weight indicates
the wish to deviate from the target value.

To give the user a better grasp of the semantics associated with each feature
the icons are responsive, in the sense that the displayed image changes in accordance with the changes of value for that feature. For instance, increasing the
average number of ants increases the number of points displayed in the corresponding icon, increasing the $avg(distance)$ increases the distance between the
start and end points of each trail, etc. Furthermore, since the features are not
independent, the changes on one value may affect the appearance of other icons;
e.g. increasing the number of ants while leaving the coverage and amount of deposited ink unchanged implies that each ant visits a smaller area of the canvas

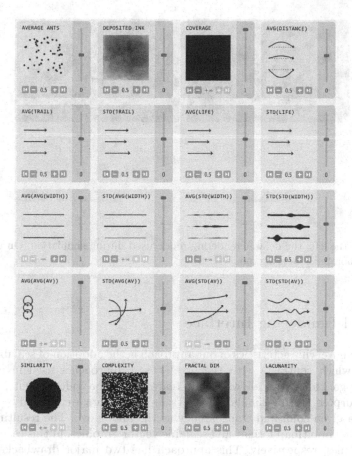

Fig. 2. The interface for fitness function design

and deposits a smaller amount of ink. The interface reflects these dependencies by decreasing the radius and opacity of the circles of the icons corresponding to deposited ink and coverage.

Figure 2 depicts the interface. The rationale behind the fitness function being specified can be described as follows: maximizing *coverage* and *similarity* promotes paintings where the ants visit the entire canvas and that closely match the original image; in what concerns line width, maximizing, $avg(std(width))$ and $std(avg(width))$ promotes high variations of width and heterogeneous widths among lines, respectively, minimizing $avg(avg(width))$ promotes thin lines; Line direction is controlled by maximizing $avg(avg(av))$ while minimizing $avg(std(av))$, which promotes the appearance of circular motifs (high angular velocity and low variation of angular velocity). The video cdv.dei.uc.pt/2014/int.mov illustrates the responsiveness of the icons.

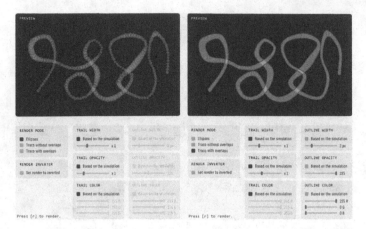

Fig. 3. On the left, the default rendering mode used during simulation. On the right, a more elaborated rendering mode.

6   Final Rendering Interface

One of the novel characteristics of our approach is the adoption of scalable vector graphics, which contrasts with the pixel based approaches used in most ant painting algorithms, and allows us to create resolution independent paintings. For this purpose, during simulation the trails of the ants are created by drawing circles of a given color and transparency as the ants move. The resulting image is then saved in bitmap format and scalable vector graphics, in this case as PNG and PDF files, respectively. This approach has two major drawbacks: (i) the PDF files may become rather large; (ii) the individual circles become visible at high zoom levels (see figure 3, left).

To overcome this problem we developed a rendering algorithm that converts the set of circles of each trail into a line of variable width. The algorithm deals with self intersecting lines and enables the specification of additional rendering options: rendering mode – default, line, line with increased opacity on self-intersections; trail width – which can be set to a given value or based on the simulation, in this case the user may specify a multiplier to increase or decrease line width; trail opacity – which has an analogous behavior to trail width; and trail color, which can be based on the simulation or set to a specific color; The user may also indicate an outline for the lines, specifying the width of the outline, its opacity and its color, which can all be specified by assigning a fixed value or by inheriting the values from the simulation (see figure 3). Finally, the invert option reverses the logic of the painting algorithm, making ants react to darkness instead of luminance.

Since the process is computationally intensive, the final rendering is typically an independent process. Once the evolutionary runs are over the users select their favorite individuals for final rendering, using the final rendering interface

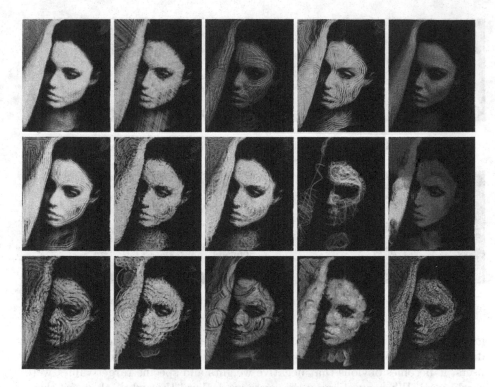

Fig. 4. Examples of phenotypes resulting from each of the 15 fitness functions

to set the rendering options. To further empower users and give them a finer degree of control, during final rendering, we allow them to add ants to points of the canvas by pointing and clicking with the mouse. Adding ants to certain regions may increase the rendering detail of that area, or introduce ants in areas of the canvas that were not being visited.

7   Experimentation

The design of our interfaces was guided by user feedback. The appearance of the icons was validated individually. For each icon we performed evolutionary runs: maximizing the value of the associated feature, minimizing it, and setting as target an intermediate value. We confronted the users with the visual outcomes of these runs and adjusted or re-designed the icons accordingly. This process was repeated interactively eventually leading to the interface described in section 5. Once developed, the fitness design interface was given to eleven users that performed multiple evolutionary runs providing additional feedback. A detailed analysis of user friendliness and user experience is beyond the scope of the paper. Nevertheless, it is worthwhile mentioning the most common complaints: (i) users are puzzled by the meaning of the negative weights; (ii) they have difficulties in

Fig. 5. The same genotype applied to different input images

Fig. 6. The same genotype rendered with different final rendering options

grasping the meaning of the fractal dimension and lacunarity icons; (iii) they dislike the similarity icon. By analyzing the fitness functions created by the users, it becomes obvious that negative weights and specific target values were rarely used. When questioning the users we realized that when they use these options their motivation was to "see what it does" rather than a specific outcome. The same applies to the use of fractal dimension and lacunarity. Considering this feedback we are likely to redefine the intervals for the weights setting them to [0,1]. The implication is that the users will no longer be able to indicate the intention to deviate from a given target value.

Giving an accurate portrayal of the results obtained by all users is close to impossible due to space limitations, therefore we focus on the results obtained by one of them: a graphic designer that was not familiar either with the inner working of the system or with the interface. After a short explanation of the workflow we asked him to create five different fitness functions and conducted ten evolutionary runs for each of these functions. Population size was set to 25 and the number of generations to 50, the other GA parameters are similar to the ones used in [11]. The input image was selected by the user, a photo of Angelina Jolie taken by Annie Leibovitz. Once these runs were finalized the user reviewed the results, selected his favorite individuals, and was asked to design an additional set of five fitness functions. This process was repeated iteratively resulting in a total of 15 fitness functions and 150 evolutionary runs. Figure 4 summarizes the results of these experiments by showing one individual per fitness function, with each row corresponding to one iteration. The results highlight not only the diversity of the results, but also the progress of the user through time.

One of the key aspects of our approach is the ability to apply selected geno-types to different input images. Thus, over time the users compile ant species that match their preferences and intentions, then applying these species to create NPRs of several images. In figure 5 we show the results of applying the genotype corresponding to the rightmost image of the bottom row of figure 4 to different input images. These results indicate that although the ant species are sensitive to the environment, i.e. input image, the characteristics of the painting, e.g. curviness of the lines, are inherent to the ant species. Therefore, applying the same ant species to different input images tends to result in ant paintings with similar aesthetic qualities.

The final rendering interface gives an additional degree of control to the users, allowing them to fine tune rendering options and explore alternative rendering modes. Figure 6 illustrates how different combinations of parameters affect the visual outcome. Since the details of the rendering are difficult to perceive in small format the video `cdv.dei.uc.pt/2014/ren.mov` illustrates the final rendering process.

8   Conclusions and Future Work

An interface for fitness function design in the scope of evolutionary ant painting system was presented. This interface allows the users to operate at a higher level of abstraction than in IEC and circumvents the user-fatigue problem. Nevertheless, unlike other automated fitness assignment schemes, the users are able to express their artistic and aesthetic preferences.

Although the system serves the user intents, different runs converge to different, and sometimes highly dissimilar, images. As such, we argue that the system opens the realm of possibilities that are consistent with the intents expressed by the users, often surprising them in the process. Moreover, while browsing the outcomes of evolutionary runs users often find images that they consider appealing due to their novelty and/or aesthetic properties, but which do not maximize the fitness function they specified. In future work we will use machine learning techniques to automatically define fitness functions from a set of such images. The automatic discovery of fitness functions may be a complement to the user interface and bring insights to understand the preferences of the users. The further refinement of the interface and the inclusion of additional features based on image analysis, more specifically related with color analysis, will also be addressed.

Acknowledgments. This research is partially funded by: QREN/COMPETE, under contract 22997 (SI & IDT-CO-PROMOÇÃO); the Portuguese Foundation for Science and Technology, project PTDC/EIA–EIA/115667/2009.

References

1. Aupetit, S., Bordeau, V., Monmarché, N., Slimane, C., Venturini, G.: Interactive Evolution of Ant Paintings. In: IEEE Congress on Evolutionary Computation, Canberra, December 8-12, vol. 2, pp. 1376–1383 (2003)
2. Collomosse, J.P.: Supervised genetic search for parameter selection in painterly rendering. In: Rothlauf, F., et al. (eds.) EvoWorkshops 2006. LNCS, vol. 3907, pp. 599–610. Springer, Heidelberg (2006)
3. Ekárt, A., Sharma, D., Chalakov, S.: Modelling human preference in evolutionary art. In: Di Chio, C., et al. (eds.) EvoApplications 2011, Part II. LNCS, vol. 6625, pp. 303–312. Springer, Heidelberg (2011)
4. Fernandes, C.M., Isidoro, C., Barata, F., Rosa, A.C., Guervós, J.J.M.: From pherographia to color pherographia: Color sketching with artificial ants. In: IEEE Congress on Evolutionary Computation. pp. 1124–1131 (2011)
5. Greenfield, G.: Evolutionary methods for ant colony paintings. In: Rothlauf, F., et al. (eds.) EvoWorkshops 2005. LNCS, vol. 3449, pp. 478–487. Springer, Heidelberg (2005)
6. Greenfield, G.: Ant Paintings using a Multiple Pheromone Model. In: Bridges, London, England (2006)
7. Hewgill, A., Ross, B.J.: Procedural 3d texture synthesis using genetic programming. Computers and Graphics 28, 569–584 (2003)
8. Karperien, A.: Fraclac for imagej, version 2.5 (2012), http://rsb.info.nih.gov/ij/plugins/fraclac/FLHelp/Introduction.htm
9. Lewis, M.: Aesthetic video filter evolution in an interactive real-time framework. In: Raidl, G.R., et al. (eds.) EvoWorkshops 2004. LNCS, vol. 3005, pp. 409–418. Springer, Heidelberg (2004)
10. Machado, P., Dias, A., Cardoso, A.: Learning to colour greyscale images. The Interdisciplinary Journal of Artificial Intelligence and the Simulation of Behaviour – AISB Journal 1(2), 209–219 (2002)
11. Machado, P., Amaro, H.: Fitness functions for ant colony paintings. In: Proceedings of the 4th International Conference on Computational Creativity, pp. 32–39 (2013)
12. Machado, P., Pereira, L.: Photogrowth: non-photorealistic renderings through ant paintings. In: Soule, T., Moore, J.H. (eds.) Genetic and Evolutionary Computation Conference, Philadelphia, PA, USA, July 7-11, pp. 233–240. ACM (2012)
13. McCormack, J.: Facing the future: Evolutionary possibilities for human-machine creativity. In: Romero, J., Machado, P. (eds.) The Art of Artificial Evolution: A Handbook on Evolutionary Art and Music, pp. 417–451. Springer (2007)
14. Monmarché, N., Mahnich, I., Slimane, M.: Artificial art made by artificial ants. In: Romero, J., Machado, P. (eds.) The Art of Artificial Evolution: A Handbook on Evolutionary Art and Music, pp. 227–247. Springer (2007)
15. Neufeld, C., Ross, B., Ralph, W.: The evolution of artistic filters. In: Romero, J., Machado, P. (eds.) The Art of Artificial Evolution: A Handbook on Evolutionary Art and Music, pp. 335–356. Springer (2007)
16. Perlin, K.: An image synthesizer. In: Cole, P., Heilman, R., Barsky, B.A. (eds.) Proceedings of the 12st Annual Conference on Computer Graphics and Interactive Techniques, SIGGRAPH 1985, pp. 287–296. ACM (1985)
17. Ramos, V.: On the implicit and on the artificial - morphogenesis and emergent aesthetics in autonomous collective systems. In: ARCHITOPIA Book, Art, Architecture and Science, pp. 25–57 (2002)

18. Ramos, V., Almeida, F.: Artificial ant colonies in digital image habitats - a mass behaviour effect study on pattern recognition. In: From Ant Colonies to Artificial Ants - 2 nd Int. Wkshp on Ant Algorithms, pp. 113–116 (2000)
19. Ross, B.J., Ralph, W., Hai, Z.: Evolutionary image synthesis using a model of aesthetics. In: Proceedings of the 2006 IEEE Congress on Evolutionary Computation, pp. 1087–1094. IEEE Press, Vancouver (2006)
20. Schlechtweg, S., Germer, T., Strothotte, T.: Renderbots – multi agent systems for direct image generation. Computer Graphics Forum 24(2), 283–290 (2005)
21. Semet, Y., O'Reilly, U.M., Durand, F.: An interactive artificial ant approach to non-photorealistic rendering. In: Deb, K., Tari, Z. (eds.) GECCO 2004. LNCS, vol. 3102, pp. 188–200. Springer, Heidelberg (2004)
22. Tzafestas, E.: Integrating drawing tools with behavioral modeling in digital painting. In: Ghandeharizadeh, S., Chang, S.F., Fischer, S., Konstan, J.A., Nahrstedt, K. (eds.) ACM Multimedia Workshops, pp. 39–42. ACM Press (2000)
23. Urbano, P.: Playing in the pheromone playground: Experiences in swarm painting. In: Rothlauf, F., et al. (eds.) EvoWorkshops 2005. LNCS, vol. 3449, pp. 527–532. Springer, Heidelberg (2005)
24. Urbano, P.: The *t. albipennis* sand painting artists. In: Di Chio, C., et al. (eds.) EvoApplications 2011, Part II. LNCS, vol. 6625, pp. 414–423. Springer, Heidelberg (2011)
25. Yip, C.: Evolving Image Filters. Master's thesis, Imperial College of Science, Technology, and Medicine (2004)

Balancing Act: Variation and Utility in Evolutionary Art

Jon McCormack

Centre for Electronic Media Art
Monash University, Caulfield East, Australia
Jon.McCormack@monash.edu
http://jonmccormack.info

Abstract. Evolutionary Art typically involves a tradeoff between the size and flexibility of genotype space and its mapping to an expressive phenotype space. Ideally we would like a genotypic representation that is terse but expressive, that is, we want to maximise the useful variations the genotype is capable of expressing in phenotype space. Terseness is necessary to minimise the size of the overall search space, and expressiveness can be loosely interpreted as phenotypes that are useful (of high fitness) and diverse (in feature space). In this paper I describe a system that attempts to maximise this ratio between terseness and expressiveness. The system uses a binary string up to any maximum length as the genotype. The genotype string is interpreted as building instructions for a graph, similar to the cellular programming techniques used to evolve artificial neural networks. The graph is then interpreted as a form-building automaton that can construct animated 3-dimensional forms of arbitrary complexity. In the test case the requirement for expressiveness is that the resultant form must have recognisable biomorphic properties and that every possible genotype must fulfil this condition. After much experimentation, a number of constraints in the mapping technique were devised to satisfy this condition. These include a special set of geometric building operators that take into account morphological properties of the generated form. These methods were used in the evolutionary artwork "Codeform", developed for the Ars Electronica museum. The work generated evolved virtual creatures based on genomes acquired from the QR codes on museum visitor's entry tickets.

Keywords: Evolutionary Art, Aesthetics, Artificial Life, genotype-phenotype mapping.

1 Introduction

A major challenge in designing evolutionary systems is defining efficient genotype representations and the phenotypes they encode for. In evolutionary art this problem is forefront when critical attention is placed on the evolutionary system and the artistic intent of what it produces.

This paper describes an artwork titled "Codeform", created by the author. The work was developed for the Ars Electronica museum in Linz, Austria, and

J. Romero et al. (Eds.): EvoMUSART 2014, LNCS 8601, pp. 26–37, 2014.

runs on the museum's *Deepspace* facility[1], a bespoke, large-scale virtual reality system with 16m × 9m stereoscopic projections onto the wall and floor using eight high-brightness stereo projectors. The space can accommodate up to several hundred participants who wear active polarising glasses to experience an immersive 3D virtual environment, generated in real-time.

1.1 Utility and Diversity

While this paper will describe the technical and implementation details of Codeform, the main purpose is to highlight a common problem for evolutionary art: achieving a good balance between the size of the genotype space and its expressive power or aesthetic[2] utility. This is a well known "open problem" for Evolutionary Music and Art [9]. In basic terms, we want a generative system that can express phenotypes that are *useful* and *diverse*. Useful in the sense that they satisfy some creative or artistic criteria (e.g. have interesting aesthetics or semantics), and diverse in the sense that they occupy distinct areas in the feature space of the phenotype. Hence we want to avoid representations that result in a large number of unappealing or highly similar phenotypes, making the evolutionary search difficult (e.g. a "needle in a haystack" problem[7, p. 21]).

In [10], this problem was described in terms of a quality factor, Q, for an evolutionary image generating system. Q was defined as the ratio between the normalised value of useful images output by the system to the size of the parameter phase-space (genotype space). A reinterpretation of this measure can be expressed:

$$Q = \frac{\nu}{\psi} \log \gamma \tag{1}$$

where ν is the total number of "interesting" phenotypes in the entire phenotype space, ψ is the total size of the phenotype space, and γ is the total size of the genotype space. The goal is to maximise Q.

"Interesting" is of course a subjective or context dependent measure and its definition can change the value of Q significantly. Here is a simple example. A 4-bit genome is used to generate integers (the phenotype) using a direct interpretation of the bit-string's integer value. If we define "interesting" as the phenotype being prime then $\nu = 7$, $\psi = \gamma = 16$, so $Q \approx 1.21$. Defining "interesting" as being divisible by 5 results in $Q \approx 0.52$. In this example the size of genotype space is equal to phenotype space due to the direct 1-to-1 mapping, but this does not need to be the general case (for any system $\psi \leq \gamma$ must be true).

Provided the definition of "interesting" is held constant, it is reasonable to compare different representation schemes in terms of their potential Q value.[3] However due to the subjective nature of its definition, comparing Q values with different criteria for "interesting" makes no sense. In the case of the work described in this paper, "interesting" has multiple dimensions and constraints.

---

[1] http://www.aec.at/center/en/ausstellungen/deep-space/
[2] "aesthetics" in the sense of 1, 2, 6 and 7 from [12].
[3] Assuming ν can be measured or estimated, which is not always possible.

Key amongst these was the requirement that all phenotypes have basic biomorphic appearances (discussed in Section 2.1), and that the aesthetic experience of the work conforms to a particular and recognisable artistic style consistent with the author's previous works.

Our goal is to maximise Q, that is to devise a system that can consistently produce useful phenotypes over the largest possible genotype space. In general terms this is often problematic because increasing the size of the genotype does not automatically result in a system that is capable of producing a higher proportion of interesting phenotypes – after a certain point the reverse is more probably the case.

This issue will be discussed in more detail in Section 3 using the Codeform artwork as the example. But before doing so we briefly review some previous work in this area, then explain Codeform's representation scheme, generative mechanism and genotype and phenotype representations.

1.2 Related Work

Many researchers have devised schemes for evolving 3D, articulated biomorphic shapes, a well-known example is that of Sims [14] who evolved virtual articulated creatures, constructed from cubic blocks, using a graph represention that coded for morphology, sensors and motor control. Hornby looked at a wide variety of representation schemes for generative design [4], including "virtual creatures" generated using a variant of L-systems. Hornby and others [2] have observed that the generative reuse of parameterised elements in encoded designs improves the ability of an evolutionary algorithm to search large design spaces. The cellular encoding technique, developed by Gruau [3] used transformational graph grammars to generate neural networks and is related to the graph-building mechanism described in this paper. Cellular encoding provided a useful generative mechanism for generating neural networks (essentially graphs), exploiting modularity and reuse in the encoding mechanism.

2 Generative Mechanisms

The project called for a simple method to convert museum visitor tickets to a unique id to use as the basis of a generative, evolutionary artificial "creature" (phenotype) that is specific to each visitor. Fortunately the tickets already had a QR code printed on them (Fig. 1), which resolved to a unique 12-digit decimal number. This number serves as both an identifier (to the ticket and its owner) and as a generator of each creature. Ticket numbering is often in sequential batches, so there was a requirement that numbers in close proximity don't generate phenotypes of similar appearance.

The ticket number was therefore used as a hash to both reference the phenotype and to generate it. Generation is a three-step transformational process:

$$ticket\ number \rightarrow genome\ string \rightarrow graph \rightarrow phenotype \qquad (2)$$

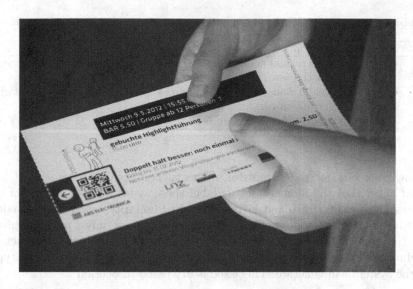

Fig. 1. Museum entry ticket showing the QR code on the left side of the ticket

To transform the ticket to the genome, the ticket number is used as the initial bit pattern in a modified linear congruential generator algorithm [6], which creates bit strings of lengths that vary between supplied minima and maxima. This ensures sufficient variation while keeping the bit string within acceptable limits. Thus the genotype generated is a bit string of length $l : l_{min} \leq l \leq l_{max}$.

The bit string genome (I) is interpreted as a series of programming instructions to a machine that builds graphs. This is somewhat similar to the cellular encoding technique developed by Gruau, which used sequences of graph transformations to build neural networks [3]. Here the instructions are represented as a binary string of machine instructions. Each instruction is 4 bits in length, consisting of a 2-bit opcode and a 2-bit parameter.

From these instructions, I, the machine, M, builds a graph $G = (N, E)$: a set of *nodes* (N) and unidirectional *edges* (E), i.e.

$$M \xrightarrow{I} G \tag{3}$$

At all times M maintains a *current node*, c, and a *root node*, r, both initially set to $\varnothing$ (empty).

Allowing 2 bits for an opcode gives 4 possible instructions, which are summarised in Table 1. Four instructions were chosen as they provide the minimum set of operations necessary to construct a graph from scratch. Opcodes 00 (add child) and 01 (add sibling) have special behaviour defined when $c = r = \varnothing$: they will add the node, n, as the root and set $c = r = n$. Instructions to create edges or shift the current node when $c = \varnothing$ are ignored.

Table 1. Instructions for the graph building machine and their interpretation

opcode	instruction	description
00pp	*add child*	add a child node of type pp to the current node (c) and set c to be the new child
01pp	*add sibling*	add a sibling node of type pp (a new child to the parent of c)
10pp	*add edge*	create an edge $c \rightarrow (c - pp) \bmod |N|$
11pp	*shift current*	set $c = (c + pp) \bmod |N|$

Allowing 2 bits for the parameter values means each node can be of four distinct types. For the moment, let us label these types A, B, C and D for the parameter values $00, 01, 10$ and 11 respectively. Similarity, when creating edges or shifting the current node the 2-bit parameter allows for only 4 possible values, being the number of nodes to move from the current node in the node set N. The choice of using only 2 parameter bits places limits on possible phenotypes that the system can generate. This issue is discussed in Section 3.

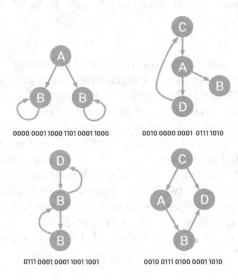

Fig. 2. Some example genome program strings and the graphs they generate

Figure 2 shows some hand-made example bit strings and the graphs they generate.

2.1 Graph Interpretation

The next stage is generating the phenotype: essentially using the graph as a generative specification for an animated 3D form. This is achieved by traversing the graph from the root node in a breadth-first traversal, interpreting information in the nodes and edges to construct time-varying 3D geometry and transformations.

Initially, we experimented with an interpretation similar to that of Sims [14], whereby each node generates a cuboid of varying dimensions with a series of articulated joints that specify the placement of the parts generated by child nodes. Sims also used a parameter to specify the "recursive limit" of node traversal to limit the number of times a node should generate a part when in a recursive cycle. Edge information was used to specify the placement of child parts relative to the parent, with child parts constrained to the surface of the parent part. Finally, a *terminal-only* flag was used to specify the connection of child parts only at the end of a recursive cycle.

These node and edge parameters were generated using the parameter information (pp) associated with each machine instruction. Having only four possible values places some limitation on the parameter variation possible, but gives enough variety to easily distinguish one phenotype from another.

This interpretation allows for a large flexibility in the structure and morphology of possible phenotypes, however for the application described in this paper there was an additional requirement: that the phenotype generated from a ticket have a basic, recognisable biomorphic appearance, including recognisable features such as lateral or radial symmetry, articulated appendage parts and a coherent overall structure. The reasons for this will be explained in Section 3.

After some experimentation, the following interpretation of the graph was used. Each node type defines a unique morphic structure, S, composed of a *connecting topology, shape* (geometry) and an ordered set of *connection points*, S_c. Connection points have specific locations over the topology that allow other structures to be connected to them and from them, subject to an affine geometric transform applied at each point. This transformation is stored as a homogeneous 4x4 matrix for each point.

Table 2. Node types and their geometric interpretation

node type		description	S
A	n-point radial symmetry	a disk shape with n radially symmetric connections	
B	bi-directional branch	branching element with laterally symmetric branch connections	
C	uni-directional branch	branching element with uni-directional laterally symmetric branch connections	
D	n−phyllotaxic	sphere with n points distributed over the surface in a phyllotaxis pattern	

Table 2 details the interpretation of each node type and shows a graphical representation of S, including the connection points, shown as either black, white or red points on an example shape (shown in grey). The difference between the black and white connection points is in the way the point performs its transformation, with the white point applying a reflection transform (lateral mirroring about the symmetry) to the child geometry instantiated at the connection point. The red point defines the location and orientation at which the structure is attached when being placed as a child object. Some examples are shown in Fig. 3. The examples in the figure show topological relationships only – additional geometric and transformational operations are also applied which are not shown in the figure for sake of clarity.

One important feature of this system is that the topologies always connect in any possible combination without generating illegal topologies or self-intersections – an important attribute given the requirement of biomorphism in every phenotype.

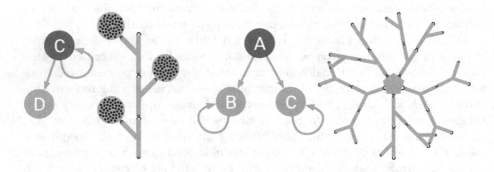

Fig. 3. Example graphs and the topological structures they generate. The root node is shown with darker shading.

The graphs are traversed using a breadth-first traversal, up to the recursive limit imposed by the node (derived from parameter information in the genome). For any given node, as each output edge is traversed an internal counter is incremented and this counter is used as an index to determine the connection point for the child object pointed to by the current edge. So if the counter value is q, the connection point is:

$$\mathcal{S}_c[q \bmod |\mathcal{S}_c|] \tag{4}$$

This means that the child node of each outgoing edge is iterated over the available connection points, the number of connections points ($|\mathcal{S}_c|$) being independent of the number of outgoing edges.

The graph traversal sends a series of commands to a 3D-turtle [1], which maintains a state, consisting of a local coordinate reference frame, transformation matrix, position, material colour, and so on. Additionally the turtle maintains a local stack and has commands to push and pop this state to and from the stack. The turtle can also instantiate geometry, so traversing the graph results in a series of commands to build a 3D geometric structure. This is a common method used in generating models from L-systems for example [5,8,13].

2.2   Animation and Sound

Connection points also include articulation information (degree of freedom, movement limits, movement function) allowing different parts of the creature to animate. Animation is performed using a simple harmonic sum-of-sines function, which is also sent as a control parameter to the sound generation system to control audio articulation.

The sound system takes control parameter and phenotype specific information (age, size, 3D position and orientation, etc.) to generate a soundscape specific to each creature. This includes generating a specific pitch contour over 8 octaves distinct to each creature and derived from the ticket number used to generate it.

Multiple creatures can exist simultaneously and sounds for each are generated individually and spatially located using a 5.1 surround speaker system. As a creature ages the pitch of the sounds it makes decrease and become slower. The sound component of the system was developed in MAX/MSP[4]. Communication with the main application via OSC over a local network. Up to fifty creatures can generate sounds simultaneously using this system. The sound system keeps track of new creatures that may begin "life" at any time, and those that die off, ending their sound-making in the system.

2.3   Evolution

As detailed at the beginning of Section 2, the visitor's ticket uniquely identifies the visitor and the phenotype (virtual creature) that the ticket generates. Visitors enter a large, immersive space and have their ticket scanned, generating the creature, which is presented to the viewer as stereoscopic 3D geometry rendered using OpenGL. Multiple tickets can be scanned, creating an ecosystem of creatures which are free to move about, breed and reproduce. Diploid reproduction is performed on each creature's bit string, I, using single point crossover constrained to instruction boundaries and bit flip mutation with probability inversely proportional to genome length/4. As the bit strings can vary in length crossover points are clamped to whichever string is shorter.

The creatures exist in a virtual 3D ecosystem, the details of which will not be covered in this paper for space reasons, but the interested reader can refer to [11] for details on the ecosystemic approach. Some important considerations are that creatures may live and die, give birth to offspring, and so on. The system is designed with a persistence mechanism and database that keeps track of all tickets scanned and all creatures generated, even those that have died. This mechanism allows for a museum visitor to return to the work at any time (from minutes to years later) and see the fate and "family tree" of their creature. Some example creatures generated from tickets are shown in Fig. 4.

---

[4] www.cycling74.com

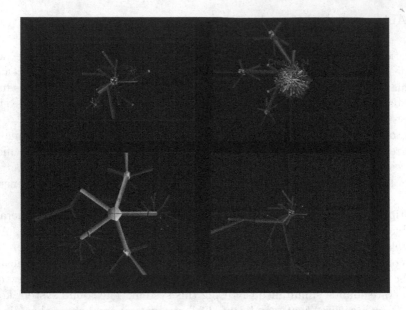

Fig. 4. Example phenotypes generated with the system (in 3D)

3   Discussion

As outlined in the introduction (Section 1), the topic of this paper is the issue of increasing the Q value from Equation 1. The size of the genotype space (γ) of the system described above is $2^{l_{max}}$. l_{max} is typically 120, making $\gamma \approx 10^{36}$, a number much larger than the 10^{12} possible ticket numbers. This is reasonable because the number of possible phenotypes is necessarily greater than the number of tickets, as genotypes can be created through evolution, not just ticket scanning (you could think of the tickets as mapping to a random initialisation point in genotype space).

One limitation of the graph generation scheme is that different genomes can potentially produce graphs of identical structure. The "add sibling" instruction can be replicated by a sequence of shifts and the "add child" instruction, similar to the way multiplication can be achieved through multiple addition nodes in a GP tree for example. However, graph structure is only one factor in phenotype generation, so two phenotypes with the same graph structure will still be different.

As discussed in Section 2.1, initially the "block creatures" method of Sims [14] was implemented as the way of interpreting the graph generated from the genome string. As is well known, Sims was able to evolve "biomorphic" creatures with characteristics strikingly reminiscent of real biology. However he was not able to get the system to evolve creatures with morphologies like those he was able to easily devise by hand, including a tree, a multi-segmented, multi-legged figure, and a human-like figure, despite these morphologies needing a maximum of only 3 nodes and 6 edges. One explanation for this difficulty is that, despite a relatively low number of elements, each node and edge contains a large number of parameters, significantly increasing the size of the search space. Additionally, certain fitness measures used (such as the distance moved from a fixed point or light following ability) would not tend to favour the evolution of tree- or human-like shapes over any others.

The application described in this paper required that when a user scans their ticket, they expect the resultant phenotype to have at least some biomorphic properties (such as those which could easily be devised by hand in Sims' system). The nature of the algorithm that converts a ticket number to genome bit-string is essentially mapping the ticket to a random point in genotype space, necessary so that consecutive ticket numbers do not produce very similar genotypes[5], as would be the case with a direct conversion of the ticket number to bit-string, for example.

Allowing only 2 parameter bits in each instruction places limitations on phenotype diversity: the translation distances in the *add edge* and *shift* instructions (Table 1) and the number of possible node types in any graph. In the case of graph generation this did not appear to be a problem. Multiple *shift* instructions, for example, allow large movements beyond the 4 possibilities allowed by a single instruction. Statistical tests on large numbers of randomly generated genotypes (bit strings) showed that increasing the parameter bits did not result in a significant increase in the variety of graph topologies generated.

While more node types could be added with an increased parameter size, this also increases the size of the search space. The question to ask is: does adding additional types significantly increase the utility *and* diversity of the resultant phenotypes? If the additional functionality gained by introducing a new type can be achieved through a combination of existing types, we are potentially increasing utility (its easier to find good phenotypes) but reducing diversity (more phenotypes will have this composite functionality).

3.1   Composing Structure

Testing the system by generating many thousands of initial bit-strings did reveal that while there was good variation in the graphs, the majority of phenotypes generated just looked like random assemblages of blocks, suggesting the value of ν from Equation 1 was very low. Trying to find even basic "biomorphic" structures that the genotype space is known to possess requires significant amounts of time to evolve, which is not practical in a situation where the time between scanning a ticket and seeing it generated must be less than around 500ms. Hence the solution is to try and increase the value of ν in Equation 1.

To achieve this the system was modified so that the nodes of the graph control a kind of "biomorphic construction kit", meaning that it will always generate

---

[5] Tickets are dispensed from rolls in sequentially numbered batches. While there are several different ticketing machines simultaneously in operation each with a different counter, analysis of ticket numbers shows that for any given audience there are many tickets that form sequences.

"acceptable" phenotypes. Interestingly, this was achieved without modification to the size of the genotype space. While this may at first seem counterintuitive, it is analogous to an evolutionary text generation system whose genome controls the assembly of words to form sentences (the phenotype). Allowing every possible word combination gives great scope, but the majority of randomly assembled words will be grammatically incorrect nonsense. Enforcing structure (adjectives precede nouns, verb conjugation, etc.) provides a good starting point for building coherent sentences.

However, by enforcing this structure, we impose a limitation on what can potentially ever evolve – nothing can "break the rules". In other words (and related to the discussion above regarding tradeoffs when increasing the number of node types), we limit the *diversity* of what is potentially possible while increasing the *utility* or usefulness of what is produced. If we equate both utility and diversity with the "interestingness" of our system (Section 1.1), then arguably we haven't increased ν as it might first have appeared. This is an inherit problem with trying to formalise the subjective, a problem that we might optimistically hope improves as our understanding of human subjectivity increases.

The experiments discussed here suggest that a system which imposes fewer structural rules has only the *potential* to generate useful diversity, not the certainty. Understanding the sizes and structure of genotype, phenotype and feature spaces allows us to make better judgments in this "balancing act" between the potential and the practical, hence improve the possible of our evolutionary art systems.

Acknowledgements. This research was supported by an Australian Research Council Discovery Project grant, DP1094064. Peter McIlwain developed the MAX/MSP sound component of the work. Thanks also to Matthew Gardiner and Benjamin Mayr from the Ars Electronica Future Lab for supporting the production of "Codeform" and to Gerfried Stocker, Director of Ars Electronica for commissioning the work.

References

1. Abelson, H., DiSessa, A.A.: Turtle geometry: the computer as a medium for exploring mathematics. The MIT Press series in artificial intelligence. MIT Press, Cambridge (1982)
2. Bentley, P.J.: Evolutionary design by computers. Morgan Kaufmann Publishers, San Francisco (1999)
3. Gruau, F.: Neural Network Synthesis using Cellular Encoding and the Genetic Algorithm. Phd thesis, l'Ecole Normale Superieure de Lyon (1994)
4. Hornby, G.S.: Generative Representations for Evolutionary Design Automation. PhD thesis, Boston, MA (2003)
5. Hornby, G.S., Pollack, J.B.: Evolving L-systems to generate virtual creatures. Computers & Graphics 26, 1041–1048 (2001)
6. Knuth, D.E.: The art of computer programming, world student series edition. World student series, vol. 2. Addison-Wesley, Reading (1972)

7. Luke, S.: Essentials of Metaheuristics. Lulu Publishing, Department of Computer Science, George Mason University (2009)
8. McCormack, J.: Aesthetic Evolution of L-Systems Revisited. In: Raidl, G.R., et al. (eds.) EvoWorkshops 2004. LNCS, vol. 3005, pp. 477–488. Springer, Heidelberg (2004)
9. McCormack, J.: Open problems in evolutionary music and art. In: Rothlauf, F., et al. (eds.) EvoWorkshops 2005. LNCS, vol. 3449, pp. 428–436. Springer, Heidelberg (2005)
10. McCormack, J.: Facing the future: Evolutionary possibilities for human-machine creativity. In: Machado, P., Romero, J. (eds.) The Art of Artificial Evolution: A Handbook on Evolutionary Art and Music, pp. 417–451. Springer (2008)
11. McCormack, J.: Creative ecosystems. In: McCormack, J., d'Inverno, M. (eds.) Computers and Creativity, ch. 2, pp. 39–60. Springer, Heidelberg (2012)
12. McCormack, J.: Aesthetics, art, evolution. In: Machado, P., McDermott, J., Carballal, A. (eds.) EvoMUSART 2013. LNCS, vol. 7834, pp. 1–12. Springer, Heidelberg (2013)
13. Prusinkiewicz, P., Lindenmayer, A.: The algorithmic beauty of plants. Number xii, 228 in The virtual laboratory. Springer, New York (1990)
14. Sims, K.: Evolving virtual creatures. In: Computer Graphics, pp. 15–22. ACM SIGGRAPH (July 1994)

Size Does Not Matter: Evolving Parameters for a Cayley Graph Visualiser Using 64 Bits

Miguel Nicolau and Dan Costelloe

Natural Computing Research & Applications Group
University College Dublin
Dublin, Ireland
miguel.nicolau@ucd.ie, dan.costelloe@gmail.com

Abstract. In this paper, an Interactive Evolutionary system is described, which generates visually appealing 3D projections of mathematical constructs. This system uses a combination of the Grammatical Evolution paradigm and Jenn3d, a visualiser of Cayley graphs of finite Coxeter groups. A very compact representation is used for the genotype strings, using only 64 bits. The resulting visualisations, albeit somewhat restricted, still exhibit a large degree of complexity and evolvability, and are well representative of the domain.

1 Introduction

One of the central aspects of evolutionary computation is the representation used. Search operators are directly related to it, and the choice of representation directly affects the effectiveness of the search (how fast can optimal solutions be found), and also the navigation of the search space, such as the degree of changes to potential solutions. In systems using mapping processes, the representation is even more crucial, as the transformations of genotype to phenotype and then to fitness can easily lose causality, leading to an essentially exploratory role of the search operators.

In an interactive evolutionary system, with an essentially user-driven evolutionary process, strong causality is of vital importance. When a user selects a given solution, and through a small change this solution is changed into a completely different one, is likely to lead to user frustration, strengthen the sense of randomness in the generative process, and ultimately cause user fatigue.

At the other extreme, a certain degree of exploration is always required, particularly in creative systems: the existence of large neutral landscapes would result in the same phenotypic solution being shown to the user multiple times, and thus also negatively affect the interactive evolutionary process.

This paper explores representational issues for a Grammatical Evolution [10] approach to the visualisation of mathematical projections. It is based on an entry to the "World in a Word" 64-Bit Design Challenge [3] (WIAW), a competition ran in conjunction with the 2013 IEEE Congress on Evolutionary Computation. The objective was to evolve 64-bit strings, which were used to explore creative

J. Romero et al. (Eds.): EvoMUSART 2014, LNCS 8601, pp. 38–49, 2014.
© Springer-Verlag Berlin Heidelberg 2014

domains. Entries were evaluated based on the originality of the domain, the diversity of the structures evolved, the appeal of the domain and the evolved individuals, and the extent to which the 64 bits were used.

There are many potential choices for the domain to explore. The competition suggested a wide range of potential areas, including visual artwork, graphic design, architectural motifs, 3D sculptures, musical styles, poetry, NLP tasks, simulations, cellular automata, games, puzzles, entire game systems, etc. Some of the examples provided include Fourier-based harmonic curves and versions of Conway's Game of Life.

Most of those domains suggested either a direct mapping, or a generative (or developmental) approach to creativity [2], such as L-Systems [6], to create as diverse structures as possible, from the (somewhat restricted) range of 64-bit strings.

The entry described here took a different approach. It used the 64 bits as a basis to create an integer string, which in turn was used with the Grammatical Evolution system [10], to evolve parameters for Jenn3d [9], a visualiser of Cayley graphs of finite Coxeter groups. The mapping process was regulated through a context-free grammar, defining the parameter space to navigate. This entry was the winner of the WIAW competition.

This is an extension of previous work [7], which created some award-winning visualisations. One won the Evolutionary Art competition at the EvoStar 2010 conference [4], and was subsequently chosen to illustrate all the proceedings associated with EvoStar 2011 [13]. Another was submitted to the prestigious *UCD Research Images* competition [1], held annually by UCD, Ireland, and finished in third place, amongst over 100 images; it is now used by the University to showcase its research programme. The use of 64 bits in this work limits the range of visualisations achievable, but still allows for an extensive exploration of the domain. It also highlights the compression potential of mapping systems such as Grammatical Evolution.

This document describes the approach taken. Section 2 gives an overview of the domain explored, and Section 3 describes the methodology used, including an overview of the evolutionary approach, the encoding used, and the fitness evaluation. Section 4 exhibits some examples generated, analyses the genotype strings evolved, and suggests further improvements.

2   Jenn3d

Jenn3d [9] is a visualiser of finite Coxeter groups on 4 elements. These groups can be represented as reflections of Euclidean 4-space, or as reflections of the 3-sphere. It builds Cayley graphs using the Todd-Coxeter algorithm, and visualizes those graphs by embedding them in the 3-sphere, then stereographically projecting the graph from the 3-sphere to Euclidean 3-space, and finally rendering the 3D structure as a 2D picture. Jenn3d renders using OpenGL, and is fast enough to allow the user to rotate and navigate in curved 3D space, and gain an intuition for the geometry of the 3-sphere.

The rich and complex domain of visualisations representable through Jenn3d is defined by the following parameters:

1. the 4×4 Coxeter matrix, as specified by the 6 integers in the upper triangle matrix;
2. a subset of up to 3 of the 4 generators, by which vertices should be fixed (the larger the subset, the fewer vertices in the quotient);
3. a list of group elements to define edges, where each element is written as a string in the generating set; and
4. a list of faces, where each face is written as a pair of generating elements.

Note that this parameter set is partial and redundant in that *(i)* most Coxeter matrices result in an infinite group and the Todd-Coxeter algorithm does not converge; *(ii)* permuting the generators results in the same structure, but with a different initial visualization; *(iii)* the lists of group elements defining edges are really sets, and so are invariant under permutation and duplication; and *(iv)* when defining edges, each group element definition can be written in infinitely many ways modulo group equality, e.g., $r_4r_4r_2r_1r_3 = r_2r_1r_3$, since $r_4r_4 = 1$ is the identity.

This large and complex parameter space of drawings is very difficult to navigate, particularly for users interested in the visualisations, but unfamiliar with Coxeter groups theory; as such, it is an excellent candidate for exploration using Grammatical Evolution.

3   Methodology

3.1   Evolutionary Approach

To explore the Jenn3d parameter space, Grammatical Evolution (GE) [10] was used. GE typically uses a variable-length Genetic Algorithm (GA) [5] to create binary or decimal strings, which choose productions from a given grammar, and thus generate syntactically correct solutions of the search space.

There are several reasons for using GE, both in the original work [7] and in the current approach. The use of grammars really simplifies the representation of the search space, allowing for an easy to use *typed* version of GP. Also, the separation of genotype and phenotype (seen in the modular view of GE, in Fig. 1) allows the usage of any search engine capable of representing numerical strings. This is crucial for the work presented here, as it means that GE could be used with a standard, fixed-length GA (with its length set to 64 bits).

Fig. 2 shows the grammar used. In it both the required and optional parameters for Jenn3d are specified. The Coxeter matrix parameter is drawn from a fixed set, as overly complex matrices are too computationally demanding, resulting in a non-convergence of the Todd-Coxeter algorithm (and hence an invalid phenotype). However, all other parameters are not only optional, but also variable in size, resulting in a large number of possible phenotype structures arising from the 64-bit encoding.

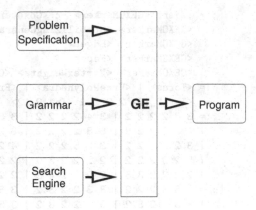

Fig. 1. Modular view of Grammatical Evolution. It combines three independent components: a problem specification (e.g., a fitness function), a grammar (syntactic representation) and a search engine (typically a variable-length genetic algorithm). The evolutionary search is performed at the level of the genotypic strings, while the fitness is evaluated on the resulting phenotype programs.

3.2   Encoding

The first step of the mapping process was to transform the 64-bit strings into integer strings. As each of these integers is used to choose productions associated to a *non-terminal* symbol defined in the grammar, the number of bits required to represent each integer is dependent on that grammar. An analysis of the grammar used (Fig. 2) shows that the symbol with the highest number of associated productions is `<FreePolyhedra>`, with 15 productions; therefore a minimum of 4 bits are required to encode each integer. The 64 bit strings are thus transformed into 16 integer strings.

Note that this introduces biases in the exploration of the phenotype space. For the `<FreePolyhedra>` symbol, for example, all productions have a 1/15 chance of being chosen, apart from the first production (`<FreePolyhedra>` → 3 3 2 2 2 2), which will have a 2/15 choice of being selected; this is due to the fact that each integer has a range of $2^4 = [0, 15]$, and GE's usage of the modulus operator to map integers to the choice of productions increases the likelihood of choosing whichever productions are first declared (unless the range of the integers used is an exact multiple of the number of production choices). GE usually deals with these biases by introducing large amounts of redundancy [11], through the use of many bits per integer (typically 32 or even 64, in systems directly manipulating integers).

Table 1 shows the number of productions associated with each grammar non-terminal symbol, and the list of probabilities of these being selected. There are 7 out of 17 symbols that exhibit some form of transformation bias, with various degrees of probability.

```
<cmdline>                   ::= ./jenn <GEXOMarker> -c <CoxeterMatrix>
                                <GEXOMarker> <StabilizingGenerators>
                                <GEXOMarker> <Edges>
                                <GEXOMarker> <Faces>
                                <GEXOMarker> <VertexWeights> <GEXOMarker>
<CoxeterMatrix>             ::= <Torus> | <FreePolyhedra> | <FreePolytope>
<Torus>                     ::= <Int_2_12> 2 2 2 <Int_2_12>
<FreePolyhedra>            ::= 3 3 2 2 2 2 | 3 4 2 2 2 2 | 3 5 2 2 2 2
                              | 4 3 2 2 2 2 | 5 3 2 2 2 2 | 3 2 3 2 2 2
                              | 3 2 4 2 2 2 | 3 2 5 2 2 2 | 4 2 3 2 2 2
                              | 5 2 3 2 2 2 | 2 2 2 2 3 3 | 2 2 2 2 3 4
                              | 2 2 2 2 3 5 | 2 2 2 2 4 3 | 2 2 2 2 5 3
<FreePolytope>             ::= 3 3 3 2 2 2 | 3 3 2 2 3 2 | 3 3 2 2 4 2
                              | 3 3 2 2 5 2 | 3 4 2 2 3 2 | 3 5 2 2 3 2
                              | 4 3 2 2 3 2 | 3 2 3 2 2 3 | 3 2 3 2 2 4
                              | 3 2 3 2 2 5 | 3 2 4 2 2 3 | 4 2 3 2 2 3
                              | 5 2 3 2 2 3 | 2 2 3 2 3 3
<StabilizingGenerators>    ::= | -v <Comb0123>
<Edges>                    ::= | -e <EdgeSet>
<EdgeSet>                  ::= <Comb0123> | <EdgeSet> <Comb0123>
<Faces>                    ::= | -f <FaceSet>
<FaceSet>                  ::= <FourInt0_3> | <FaceSet> <FourInt0_3>
<FourInt0_3>               ::= <Int0_3>
                              | <Int0_3><Int0_3>
                              | <Int0_3><Int0_3><Int0_3>
                              | <Int0_3><Int0_3><Int0_3><Int0_3>
<VertexWeights>            ::= | -w <Int1_12> <Int1_12> <Int1_12> <Int1_12>
<Int0_3>                   ::= 0 | 1 | 2 | 3
<Int1_12>                  ::= 1 | 2 | 3 | 4 | 5 | 6 | 7 | 8 | 9
                              | 10 | 11 | 12
<Int2_12>                  ::= 2 | 3 | 4 | 5 | 6 | 7 | 8 | 9
                              | 10 | 11 | 12
<Int3_12>                  ::= 3 | 4 | 5 | 6 | 7 | 8 | 9
                              | 10 | 11 | 12
<Comb0123>                 ::= 0 | 1 | 2 | 3
                              | 01 | 02 | 03 | 12 | 13 | 23
                              | 012 | 013 | 023 | 123 | 0123
```

Fig. 2. Grammar used to navigate the Jenn3d parameter space

Also note that not all 2^{64} possible binary strings generate unique individuals. Some do not generate valid phenotypes at all, as the mapping process might not terminate; others generate the same choices in the grammar, and hence the same phenotypes; and finally some combinations of the leftmost bits will generate shorter mappings, which will not use some of the rightmost bits.

Even so, the number of possible combinations is still very large, and the functionality of each bit can vary, depending on the production choices of the

Table 1. Probabilities of non-terminal symbol mapping transformations, using 4 bits to encode each choice

Nonterminal Symbol	Choices	Mapping Transformation Probabilities
<cmdline>	1	100%
<CoxeterMatrix>	3	37.5%, 31.25%, 31.25%
<Torus>	1	100%
<FreePolyhedra>	15	12.5%, 6.25% .. 6.25%
<FreePolytope>	14	12.5%, 12.5%, 6.25% .. 6.25%
<StabilizingGenerators>	2	50%, 50%
<Edges>	2	50%, 50%
<EdgeSet>	2	50%, 50%
<Faces>	2	50%, 50%
<FaceSet>	2	50%, 50%
<FourInt0_3>	4	25%, 25%, 25%, 25%
<VertexWeights>	2	50%, 50%
<Int0_3>	4	25%, 25%, 25%, 25%
<Int1_12>	12	12.5%, 12.5%, 12.5%, 12.5%, 6.25% .. 6.25%
<Int2_12>	11	12.5%, 12.5%, 12.5%, 12.5%, 12.5%, 6.25% .. 6.25%
<Int3_12>	10	12.5% .. 12.5%, 6.25%, 6.25%, 6.25%, 6.25%
<Comb0123>	15	12.5%, 6.25% .. 6.25%

bits preceding it. Furthermore, from a visualisation point of view, the search space is potentially infinite, as the user can select from a multitude of rotation and zoom combinations for each visualisation.

Efficient Exploitation. A custom GA is used, along with extensions in GE, to introduce crossover markers through the grammar [8]. This technique is especially useful when domain knowledge allows the apriori identification of blocks of information: special non-terminal symbols are introduced in the grammar, and the GA is then limited to these crossover points. It has been used in the past to separate well-defined behaviours for video controllers [12], and also in the previous application of GE to Jenn3d [7]; previous work has even allowed these crossover markers to evolve their position [8].

The crossover point markers used in this study can be seen in the grammar (Fig. 2), in the <cmdline> non-terminal symbol declaration. A special <GEXOMarker> symbol was inserted between each parameter set; these allowed those sets to be exchanged between individuals, thus increasing the visual relationship between parents and offspring.

Note that the Java framework provided for the competition [3] also uses a Monte-Carlo (MC) algorithm [14] as a search procedure. This however is incompatible with the representation used, because deep explorations typical of MC search (i.e. explorations of the rightmost bits in the bit string) can potentially always generate the same visualisation; this is particularly true for bit strings where the mapping process does not use the whole genotype string. As such, the MC algorithm was not used.

3.3   Fitness Evaluation

As the objective of the system is to evolve attractive and personalised visualisations, it runs in an interactive manner. Each correctly generated individual is exposed to the user, to receive a fitness score. This allows the individual to directly interact with the 3D-visualisation, have a better understanding of the generated structure, and achieve his/her preferred projection, before assigning a fitness score.

Fig. 3 shows the Jenn3D interface, extended so that a scoring process is present. Ideally, the evolutionary process proceeds in an endless manner; every time a fitness score is attributed to a structure, a new one is presented immediately after. If the user instead chooses to *exit* the application, the evolutionary process terminates. The full range of exploration tools in Jenn3d is available for each presented structure; this includes options to save the evolved parameters, and/or export a high-resolution image of the current visualisation.

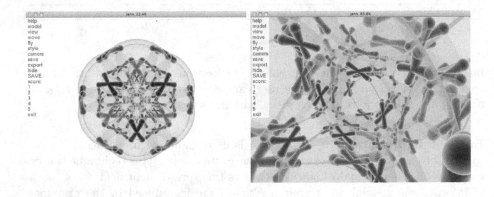

Fig. 3. The Jenn3d interface, along with the extensions encoded. An example structure is shown in the left; the same structure, when zoomed in and rotated (right), can produce a dramatically different visualisation.

Fitness and Typicality. Alongside a fitness score (in the range $[0.0, 5.0]$), the competition also required a *typicality* value in the range $[0.0, 1.0]$, indicating how well an individual represents the domain (typically a functional measure that captures some key structural properties). In the case of Jenn3d, it is not intuitively obvious how to set this score, as structural analysis of the generated visualisations is not possible, and hence the range of typicality values was limited.

Table 2 shows the range of possible fitness and typicality scores. Due to the complexity of the Todd-Coxeter algorithm, some visualisations are impossible to generate, causing the Jenn3d software to crash[1]; as these might be close to correct (and potentially attractive) visualisations, fitness and typicality scores of 0.5 are automatically attributed.

Table 2. Fitness and Typicality scores, and events generating those scores; fitness values 1-5 are user supplied

Event	Fitness	Typicality
Unsuccessful GE mapping	0.0	0
Non-convergence of Tedd-Coxeter algorithm	0.5	0.5
Rejected visualisation	1.0	1.0
Poor visualisation score	2.0	1.0
Average visualisation score	3.0	1.0
High visualisation score	4.0	1.0
Visualisation remains in population unchanged	5.0	1.0

The user can control the evolutionary process through the fitness score. A fitness score of 1.0, for example, guarantees that the current visualisation is replaced by a random one in the next generation, whereas a score of 5.0 guarantees that the visualisation is passed unchanged to the next generation, thus potentially being used as a seed for alternative, similar visualisations (as per the scoring process proposed previously [7]).

4   Results

Table 3 shows example projections, achieved through evolution, along with their hexadecimal, integer and mapped strings. The specific visualisations were chosen to the taste of the authors. Higher resolution images are shown in Fig. 4.

These examples also show the variety with which the bit strings are used. The 2nd, 3rd and 4th solutions, for example, came from the same evolutionary run, and their similar parameter structure still exhibits traces of the genetic material exchanged through marked crossover (and subsequently altered by mutation); the resulting projections are however substantially different. The 7th solution (0xdb400f50dc50f13a), on the other hand, illustrates how some solutions can be very small, by using only 40 bits to encode its solution (i.e. it has a tail of 24 unused bits).

4.1   More Efficient Encoding

Although the encoding used allows a vast exploration of the domain, there is still room for improvement. A variable number of bits per integer can be used, as the

---

[1] This can be frustrating for the user, and a workaround in the Jenn3d software is beyond the scope of this study (and the mathematical knowledge of the authors); a smart way to deal with this problem (in a Mac environment) is to leave the crash report window open, as only a single such window can be open at any given time.

Table 3. Parameters evolved for the examples shown in Fig. 4

	Hex: 0x9134db20eb2d6f07 Genotype: 9 1 3 4 13 11 2 0 14 11 2 13 6 15 0 7 Phenotype: jenn -c 3 2 2 2 2 5 -e 0 0123 -f 23
	Hex: 0x53090ffede18f1b8 Genotype: 5 3 0 9 0 15 15 14 13 14 1 8 15 1 11 8 Phenotype: jenn -c 3 3 2 2 5 2 -e 0 -f 21
	Hex: 0xc3298ff8d8003028 Genotype: 12 3 2 9 8 15 15 8 13 8 0 0 3 0 2 8 Phenotype: jenn -c 5 2 2 2 2 4 -v 13 -e 123 13
	Hex: 0xc3090fe89c10f098 Genotype: 12 3 0 9 0 15 14 8 9 12 1 0 15 0 9 8 Phenotype: jenn -c 5 2 2 2 2 2 -v 0 -e 13 -f 03
	Hex: 0xdb410f50dc59f1ba Genotype: 13 11 4 1 0 15 5 0 13 12 5 9 15 1 11 10 Phenotype: jenn -c 2 2 2 2 3 4 -e 0 -f 01 -w 4 2 12 11
	Hex: 0xd1410f70dc59f0ac Genotype: 13 1 4 1 0 15 7 0 13 12 5 9 15 0 10 12 Phenotype: jenn -c 3 4 2 2 2 2 -e 0 -f 01 -w 4 1 11 1
	Hex: 0xdb400f50dc50f13a Genotype: 13 11 4 0 0 15 5 0 13 12 5 0 15 1 3 10 Phenotype: jenn -c 2 2 2 2 3 4 -w 6 1 2 1
	Hex: 0xd2410ef0d859f4be Genotype: 13 2 4 1 0 14 15 0 13 8 5 9 15 4 11 14 Phenotype: jenn -c 3 5 2 2 2 2 -e 0123 -f 01 -w 4 5 12 3

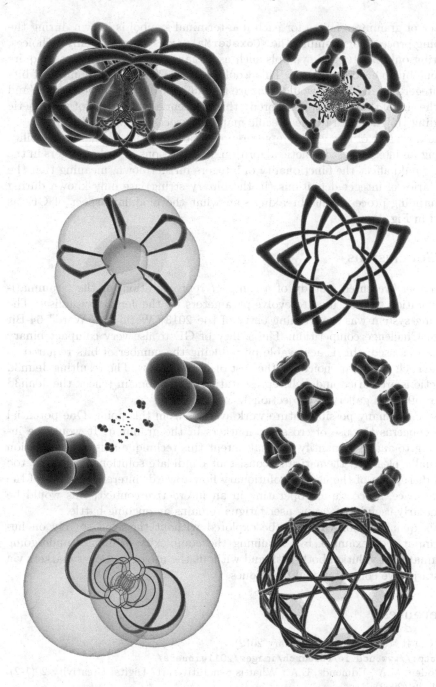

Fig. 4. Mapping examples

number of grammar choices for each non-terminal symbol is known during the mapping process: for example, the <CoxeterMatrix> symbol has only 3 choices, requiring only 2 bits, and symbols such as <StabilizingGenerators> require only one bit to encode a choice. This would decrease the average number of bits per integer, which in turn would increase the number of integers generated (and thus the size of the landscape explored); this is essentially a version of Arithmetic Encoding [15], adapted to the specific mapping process employed by GE.

The downside of this very compact representation would be the impossibility of using an integer-based genetic algorithm, as mutations in early integers in the string would affect the functionality of integers further down, meaning that the boundaries of integer definitions (in the binary string) are only known during the mapping process (thus breaking somewhat the modular aspect of GE, as shown in Fig. 1).

5 Conclusions

This paper presented a study of a compact representation for the Grammatical Evolution system, used to evolve parameters for the Jenn3d visualiser. The resulting system was the winning entry of the 2013 "World in a Word" 64-Bit Design Challenge competition. The ability of GE to use very compact binary strings was used; this is achievable by reducing the number of bits required to encode each grammar choice (at the cost of some biases). The resulting Jenn3d projections are varied and well representative of the domain (check the Jenn3d website [9] for a gallery of projections).

There are many possible future work avenues from this point. One potential route concerns the use of crossover markers in the grammar. It would be interesting to analyse/quantify to what extent this technique aids the generation of visually pleasing, thematically consistent candidate solutions – without too much disruption of the user's evolutionary flow towards interesting areas of the search space. Since we are operating in an interactive context, this would be particularly useful as fighting user-fatigue remains an ongoing battle.

This quantification can even be explored without the need to rely on human input. For example, by examining the complexity of images undergoing Grammatical Evolution both with and without the use of crossover markers via non-subjective computational techniques.

References

1. UCD Research Images (February 2012),
   http://www.ucd.ie/research/images/2011winners/
2. Boden, M.A., Edmonds, E.A.: What is generative art? Digital Creativity 20(1-2), 21–46 (2009)
3. Browne, C.: World in a word 64-bit design challenge (June 2013),
   http://www.cameronius.com/research/cec/
4. Esparcia-Alcázar, A.I., Ekárt, A., Silva, S., Dignum, S., Uyar, A.Ş. (eds.): EuroGP 2010. LNCS, vol. 6021, pp. 1–13. Springer, Heidelberg (2010)

5. Holland, J.H.: Adaptation in Natural and Artificial Systems. University of Michigan Press (1975)
6. Lindenmayer, A.: Mathematical models for cellular interaction in development, parts i and ii. Journal of Theoretical Biology 18, 280–315 (1968)
7. Nicolau, M., Costelloe, D.: Using grammatical evolution to parameterise interactive 3d image generation. In: Di Chio, C., Brabazon, A., Di Caro, G.A., Drechsler, R., Farooq, M., Grahl, J., Greenfield, G., Prins, C., Romero, J., Squillero, G., Tarantino, E., Tettamanzi, A.G.B., Urquhart, N., Uyar, A.Ş. (eds.) EvoApplications 2011, Part II. LNCS, vol. 6625, pp. 374–383. Springer, Heidelberg (2011)
8. Nicolau, M., Dempsey, I.: Introducing grammar based extensions for grammatical evolution. In: Proceedings of the IEEE Congress on Evolutionary Computation, CEC 2006, Vancouver, BC, Canada, July 16-21, pp. 2663–2670. IEEE Press (2006)
9. Obermeyer, F.: Jenn3d for visualizing coxeter polytopes (June 2010), http://jenn3d.org
10. O'Neill, M., Ryan, C.: Grammatical Evolution - Evolutionary Automatic Programming in an Arbitrary Language. Genetic Programming, vol. 4. Kluwer Academic (2003)
11. O'Neill, M., Ryan, C., Nicolau, M.: Grammar defined introns: An investigation into grammars, introns, and bias in grammatical evolution. In: Spector, L. (ed.) Proceedings of the Genetic and Evolutionary Computation - GECCO 2001, Genetic and Evolutionary Computation Conference, San Francisco, CA, USA, July 7-11, pp. 97–103. Morgan Kaufmann (2001)
12. Perez, D., Nicolau, M., O'Neill, M., Brabazon, A.: Evolving behaviour trees for the mario ai competition using grammatical evolution. In: Di Chio, C., et al. (eds.) EvoApplications 2011, Part I. LNCS, vol. 6624, pp. 123–132. Springer, Heidelberg (2011)
13. Silva, S., Foster, J.A., Nicolau, M., Machado, P., Giacobini, M. (eds.): EuroGP 2011. LNCS, vol. 6621. Springer, Heidelberg (2011)
14. Sutton, R.S., Barto, A.G.: Reinforcement Learning: An Introduction. MIT Press (1998)
15. Witten, I.H., Neal, R.M., Cleary, J.G.: Arithmetic coding for data compression. Communications of the ACM 30(6), 520–540 (1987)

A Complexity Approach for Identifying Aesthetic Composite Landscapes

Adrian Carballal, Rebeca Perez, Antonino Santos, and Luz Castro

Department of Information and Communication Technologies
University of A Coruña, A Coruña, Spain
{adrian.carballal,rebeca.perezf,nino,maria.luz.castro}@udc.es

Abstract. The present paper describes a series of features related to complexity which may allow to estimate the complexity of an image as a whole, of all the elements integrating it and of those which are its focus of attention. Using a neural network to create a classifier based on those features an accuracy over 85% in an aesthetic composition binary classification task is achieved. The obtained network seems to be useful for the purpose of assessing the Aesthetic Composition of landscapes. It could be used as part of a media device for facilitating the creation of images or videos with a more professional aesthetic composition.

1 Introduction

An evaluator which enable users without an artistic background to take pictures of better appearance could be used by different multimedia devices. It could help users to identify in real time those framings with a certain aesthetic value. It could be also used for different tasks related to aesthetic composition: identification, classification, categorization, etc.; both in real-time multimedia devices and in stand-alone applications.

Unlike those systems which allow access to the images intrinsic information based on different image phenomena, such as contrast, determine the aesthetic composition of a given image is not a trivial task.

Numerous papers [9,16,11] have appeared in recent years evaluating different elements of the aesthetic value of images and different ways to estimate it. This paper introduces the uses of different metrics based on those works, based on the complexity of an image, which have already proven useful in experiments related to the ordering and classification based on stylistic and aesthetic criteria [15,8,13,14]. These metrics and their usefulness for calculating the aesthetic composition of a landscape is studied.

The present paper is structured as follows: i) a short description of the state of the art in composition systems is included; ii) a set of complexity metrics and their usefulness for calculating the aesthetic composition of a landscape is presented and the features to be used in the study are described; iii) the results obtained in an experiment of image classification according to their aesthetic composition are shown; iv) the overview of a photography expert about the results is shown; v) and, finally, the conclusions and the upcoming research lines for improving the already presented approach will be explained.

J. Romero et al. (Eds.): EvoMUSART 2014, LNCS 8601, pp. 50–61, 2014.
© Springer-Verlag Berlin Heidelberg 2014

2   State of the Art

Previous works focus on the search for metrics which show the composition quality or cropping methods which enhance the visual and aesthetic quality of a given image. Most of them use metrics related to Rule of Thirds (RoT) [5], Region of Interest (ROI) [21], or Saliency [17] individually. RoT is a photographic framing technique which divides the scene into 9 equally sized parts by means of three vertical and horizontal equidistant lines. This technique is based on placing the heaviest elements at the intersection among these lines. On the other hand, the use of ROI determines those image areas grouping the elements which attract the greatest interest. Saliency detection allows the differentiation of a foreground object from the background and to classify it as an interesting point.

Santella et al. [17] presented a system which records user's eye movements for a few seconds to identify important image content. The given approach is capable of generating crops of any size or aspect ratio. The main disadvantage is that the system incurs on requiring user input, so it can't be considered a fully-computational approach. Once the important area of an image is detected, the crops are made considering three basics on photography: (i) include an entire subject and some context around, (ii) edges should pass through featureless areas whenever possible, (iii) the area of the subject matter should be maximized to increase clarity. They presented 50 images cropped using 3 different approaches: saliency-based [18], professional hand-crop, and gaze-crop to 8 different subjects. They obtained that their gaze-based approach was preferred to saliency-based cropping in 58.4% of trials and in 32.5% to professional cropping.

Liu et al. [5] have translated several basic composition guidelines into quantitative aesthetic scores, including the Rule of Thirds, diagonal, visual balance, and region size. Based on which, an automatic crop-and-retarget approach to producing a maximally beautiful version of the input image. Their approach searches for the optimal composition result in a 4D space which contains all cropped windows with various widths and heights. A dataset of 900 casual images arbitrarily collected from international websites in which skilled photographers rank photographs through them was employed to evaluate their score function. To evaluate the performance of their method generated a set of 30 triplets of images; the original image, one crop using Santella's method and one using theirs. These triplets were shown to 56 subjects, males and women, between 21 and 55 years old. In 44.1% of cases, the subjects preferred the cropped images provided by their approach. In addition, 81.8% were not able to distinguish whether the image was hand-cropped or computationally optimized.

Wang and Cohen [19] propose an algorithm for composing foreground elements onto a new background by integrating matting and compositing into a single process. The system is able to compose more efficiently and with fewer artifacts compared with previous approaches. The matte is optimized in a sense that it will minimize the visual artifacts on the final composed image, although it may not be the true matte for the foreground. They determine the size and position that minimizes the difference between a small shell around the foreground and the new background, and then run the compositional matting. The developed algorithm not always gives satisfying compositions when the new background differs significantly from the original.

Zhang et al. [21] presented an auto-cropping model to obtain an optimal cropped image using the width and height of the original image, the conservative coefficient, the faces detected and the Region of Interest (ROI). The model consists of three sub models: (i) a composition sub model to describe how good the composition is, (ii) a conservative sub model to prevent the photograph from being cropped too aggressively and (iii) a penalty factor to prevent faces or ROIs being cut off. They used 100 pictures randomly selected from 600 home photographs. All the images were used into two studies. The first user study evaluated the auto cropping result in different aspect ratios. They obtained that the algorithm exhibits a satisfactory score on cropping. The second user study evaluated the improvement of the picture composition after cropping, in which observed the considering of the artistic rules leads to a good score of the improvement of the picture composition.

Suh et al. [18] proposed a set of fully automated image cropping techniques using a visual salience model based on low-level contrast measures. According to them, the more salient a portion of image, the more informative it is; and the visual search performance is increased as much recognizable the thumbnail is. They used their feature set on recognizing objects in small thumbnails (Recognition Task) and to measure how the thumbnail generation technique affects search performance (Visual Search Task). They ran an empirical study over 20 subjects, which were college or graduate students at the University of Maryland, and 500 filler images. In both tasks, the proposed set was capable to provide thumbnails substantially more recognizable and easier to find in the context of visual search.

What if the quality of aesthetic composition may be related to the visual complexity of the composition itself, as well as to the complexity derived from each of the elements represented in the same image? We assume that, inside the images, there are elements which attract the observer's attention and their complexity must be taken into account when determining the composition aesthetics. This assumption takes into account what Philip Galanter calls "effective complexity" [3]. According to him, an artist will tire both high ordered and high disordered aesthetic composition because of lack any structural complexity worth. We propose the joint use of metrics which allow to estimate the complexity of an image as a whole, as well as of all the elements integrating it and, particularly, those which are its focus of attention. Following this hypothesis, this work will centre concretely on the study of the aesthetic composition of landscapes. The proposed metrics are listed next.

3   Complexity Metrics and Presented Features

Machado and Cardoso [9], based on previous works by [1], proposes JPEG and FRACTAL compression methods to estimate the image complexity. On [2] it is found a correlation between compression error and complexity of the image.

The error involved in the JPEG compression method, which affects mainly to high frequencies, depends on the variability of the pixels in the image. From this point of view, more variability involves more randomness and therefore more complexity. The FRACTAL method tends to compress an image by filtering the self-similarities within. In this case, more self-similarities implies less variability, and therefore less complexity. Hence we considered applying JPEG and FRACTAL Compression methods as image complexity estimatives.

Since both are lossy compression schemes, there might be a compression error, i.e., the compressed image will not exactly match the original. Three levels of detail for the JPEG and FRACTAL compression metrics are considered: low, medium and high. More info available at [14].

Salience is the quality that stands out one or multiple important objects from those that surrounds it/them. Somehow, saliency facilitates to focus the perception of the viewer on the most pertinent item or items on a scene. The saliency algorithm chosen to implement was the Subject Saliency algorithm also known as Subject Region Extraction [6]. Based on the idea that the subject in a photograph would be clearer and the background would be blurred, the algorithm extracts the clear region of an image which theoretically holds the subject. This algorithm uses images statistics to detect 2D blurred regions in an image, based on a modification of [4] work. Subject Salience will be used to detect the foreground item/s, which should get the focus of attention.

The Sobel Filter calculates the gradient of the image intensity at each point, giving the direction of the greater variation from light to dark and the amount of variation in that same direction. This gives us an idea of the variation of brightness at each point, from smooth to sharp differences. With this filter it is estimated the presence of the light-dark transitions and how they are oriented. With these light-dark variations corresponding to the intense and well-defined boundaries between objects, it is possible to obtain edge detection. The Sobel Filter will give a simple representation of all the elements standing on the image by identifying their silhouettes.

We have also chosen to use a set of basic features related to the statistical variability of the pixels integrating an image. Said features calculate: (i) the mean (ii) and the standard deviation of the pixels with regard to the adjacent pixels in each color channel.

It must be explained the way in which our features set will be obtained. Four auxiliary images are generated from every image. Three of those images are obtained by separating the color channels following the HSV model. The fourth image stems from an attempt to solve the existing problems of the HSV color model for the extreme values of the H and V channels. When pixel value of $V = 0$ the resulting color is always black. In the case of $S = 0$ then the resulting color is always in grayscale. Another problem occurs when $V = 255$ and $S = 0$, in which the color is white. In any of these situations it can not be assured that data from H are correct as it depends directly from the transformation algorithm to HSV format. In an attempt to address this deficiency, a new image is determined by multiplying pixel by pixel the S and V channels within the range [0, 255]. It will be referred to from now on as CS or Colorfulness [12].

Splitting the image in mentioned color channels and applying the complexity metrics to each of the resulting images gives a total of 24 features (from now feature set COMPLEX). It must be noted that these 24 features will be calculated based on the original image, having applied the Subject Saliency and the Sobel Filter again. Therefore, we will achieve a total number of 72 features (set COMPLEX^F). Since Hue channel is circular, the mean and standard deviation are calculated based on the angle values of Hue and its norm. In addition, it is performed the multiplication of the Hue angle by the pixel intensity values of CS, and a new value of the norm is calculated using values from H and CS. It yields another 12 features per image (from now set BASE), 7 related with mean (set AVG) and 5 related with standard deviation (set STD), giving another set of 36 features per image if also applying Subject Saliency and Sobel Filter (set BASE^F).

4   Experimental Dataset for Aesthetic Composition

A total of 1961 landscape images of high aesthetic quality in their composition have been compiled for carrying out this experiment, most of them wallpapers in landscape format. All of them have a resolution higher than 1024x1024 pixels. Their visual topics vary a great deal: night, day, mountain, beach, etc.

From this initial dataset, a random algorithm was created which will provide sub-images with a width/height ratio equal to the original image (see functioning in Algorithm 1). Said algorithm has been used on every image, thus providing a second set of images of the same sampling size.

A photography expert has identified those images which, because of the random cropping, generated a new image which was equal or better than the original one as regards framing. All these images have been discarded, achieving a final dataset integrated by two sets of 1757 images each.

Figure 1 shows a simple subset of images of both sets. The left side shows images of the original set, while the right side shows the same subset once the algorithm has been applied.

5   Classification Method and Results Obtained

Both images to be used in this experimental part and the features which will characterize them individually have been presented so far. The present section explains the experiment carried out.

A classification model has been developed using SNNS (Stuttgart Neural Network Simulator) [20]. In particular, a backpropagation MLP is used with 3-layer architecture: an input layer with 108 neurons, a single hidden layer of 15 neurons and an output layer with 1 neuron. This configuration has been established based on previous experiments and experiences of the research team in tasks of the same field [10,7].

Algorithm 1. Random Image Cropping

---

1 **for** *each image* **do**
2 | A random height is established (between 400px and 1/2 of the height of the original image)
3 | A width is established according to the ratio of the original image
4 | Random locx and locy are created (< 0, $>$ original size)
5 | **if** *the cropped image does not exceed the original on the right or at the bottom:* **then**
6 | | accept cropping
7 | **else**
8 | | return to 2

The network training will finish when a maximum number of 1000 cycles is reached. The initial network weights are determined at random within the range [-0.1, 0.1]. A maximum error tolerance of 0.3 has been used. The 10-fold Cross-Validation (10-fold CV) model has been used for the generation of the training data sets so that their results are statistically relevant. Each of these runs has a different training and validation set which have been randomly generated. The results shown correspond to the average results obtained in these 10 runs.

Given that the neural network provides a number value within the range of 0 and 1, a binary system has been used for cataloguing the images. Those images which have a network output, once they have been presented to the system, of less than 0.5 will be catalogued as having a low aesthetic composition. The classification results given for each feature set presented in Section 3 are shown in Table 1.

Table 1. Precision and Recall using ANNs

Feature Set	#feats	Accuracy	RECALL		PRECISION	
			Cropped	Original	Cropped	Original
COMPLEX^F	72	85.74%	82.64%	88.84%	88.11%	83.65%
COMPLEX	24	80.88%	76.49%	85.26%	83.84%	78.39%
BASE^F	36	78.66%	73.99%	83.32%	81.61%	76.21%
BASE	12	75.67%	69.04%	82.30%	79.59%	72.66%
AVG	7	71.60%	68.70%	74.50%	72.93%	70.41%
STD	5	74.67%	67.79%	81.56%	78.61%	71.69%

According to the data, it may be seen that the image classification when using the BASE set seems to achieve relatively satisfactory results. It should be noted that the problem itself contributes to the achievement of such high results. Let's imagine that there is a landscape photography similar to the one in Figure 2a. Having applied the random cropping, the new image may result as the one seen in Figure 2c.

(a) Original image 1

(b) Cropped image 1'

(c) Original image 2

(d) Cropped image 2'

(e) Original image 3

(f) Cropped image 3'

(g) Original image 4

(h) Cropped image 4'

Fig. 1. Example images of both sets (images of the original set on the left and the cropped version on the right)

(a) Original Image   (b) Cropping Selection

(c) Resulting Image

Fig. 2. Cropping example

In this case, as is usually the case in this kind of images, the cropped landscapes usually have an extreme pixel variability compared to the original image. That is, the mean and the standard deviation of the pixels integrating the resulting image either increases or decreases considerably. Anyhow, no element of the real content of any of the two images is taken into account for the classification.

The network trained with $COMPLEX^F$ set offers a success rate of 85.74%. Individually, the network succeeds 88.84% of the original set versus 82.64% of cropped one. Considering precision, we obtained a rate of 83.66% relative to originals and 88.11% relative to cropped images. The results seem to be well-balanced globally, both in accuracy and precision.

The fact of not using edge detection filters (COMPLEX set) derives in a decrease in both recall and precision, which demonstrates that to attend to the important elements present on a landscape provides relevant information. On the other hand, if we compare with $BASE^F$ is seen as a lesser set of complexity metrics provide better results than the filters applied on different measures of variability of the pixels.

The observed results seem to indicate that to attend to the complexity of the important elements inside a landscape allow to differentiate those images that present a better composition.

5.1   An Expert Overview

The mentioned expert was presented with the images which the classifier was and wasn't capable of identifying correctly, without having any kind of information about the method used.

According to the expert, the classifier seems to work correctly in those not obvious cases where there is some element of brightness, light or where the differentiating element is relatively small with regard to the image (Figure 3a). Even on those images whose content bears a great symmetry, regardless of their content or originality (Figure 3b).

(a) Small differentiating element   (b) Symmetry regardless content

Fig. 3. Examples of well classified images

In case of false positives, one of the most frequent mistakes happens when the system cannot find any differentiating element in the image (Figure 4a). The resulting image after applying the Sobel Filter seems to contain a lot of noise compared to those images where there is a clear differentiator that the edge detector identifies correctly (Figure 4b).

On the contrary, false negative cases, sometimes the mistake is perfectly justified: cropped image pieces partially comply with the principles of framing; they structure a differentiating element at the center while their environment goes totally unnoticed as a uniform background (Figure 5).

The expert concluded that most of the mistakes generated by the presented classification method were not trivial and were sometimes understandable.

| (a) Applying no filter | (b) Applying Sobel Filter |

Fig. 4. Example of a wrongly classified image because of the Sobel Filter

| (a) Original | (b) Cropped |

Fig. 5. Example of a wrongly classified image as original being cropped

6   Future Work

This paper has presented a set of metrics based on complexity which seem to be useful for judging the aesthetic composition in landscape images. A neural network has been used as a binary classifier using the presented features as inputs, achieving accuracy and precision results over 85%.

This classifier could be add to any real-time multimedia device and used for different tasks related to aesthetic composition like identification or classification, categorization, etc. For this propose we intend to modify the classification system so that asynchronous tasks can be performed by means of parallel programming, thus reducing the time of the task of extracting metrics from each image, which currently entails the biggest bottleneck.

Among the most immediate enhancements, we may mention above all the elimination of all those cases identified by the expert where the classifier fails, both in the case of false positives and negatives. For this purpose, we intend to search for another set of metrics which can help the already existing one with that task, and even to find alternatives for Sobel and Saliency Subjects, so that their detection problems do not have a direct impact on the prototype.

Acknowledgments. This research was partially funded by: Xunta de Galicia, project XUGA-PGIDIT 10TIC105008PR and the Portuguese Foundation for Science and Technology, project PTDC/EIA-EIA/115667/2009.

References

1. Arnheim, R.: Art and Visual Perception, a Psychology of the Creative Eye. Faber and Faber, London (1956)
2. Forsythe, A., Nadal, M., Sheehy, N., Cela-Conde, C.J., Sawey, M.: Predicting beauty: Fractal dimension and visual complexity in art. British Journal of Psychology 102(1), 49–70 (2011)
3. Galanter, P.: What is generative art? complexity theory as a context for art theory. In: International Conference on Generative Art, Milan, Italy (2003)
4. Levin, G., Feinberg, J., Curtis, C.: Alphabet synthesis machine (2006), http://alphabet.tmema.org
5. Liu, L., Chen, R., Wolf, L., Cohen-Or, D.: Optimizing photo composition. Comput. Graph. Forum 29(2), 469–478 (2010)
6. Luo, Y., Tang, X.: Photo and video quality evaluation: Focusing on the subject. In: Forsyth, D., Torr, P., Zisserman, A. (eds.) ECCV 2008, Part III. LNCS, vol. 5304, pp. 386–399. Springer, Heidelberg (2008)
7. Machado, P., Cardoso, A.: All the truth about NEvAr. Applied Intelligence, Special Issue on Creative Systems 16(2), 101–119 (2002)
8. Machado, P., Romero, J., Cardoso, A., Santos, A.: Partially interactive evolutionary artists. New Generation Computing – Special Issue on Interactive Evolutionary Computation 23(42), 143–155 (2005)
9. Machado, P., Cardoso, A.: Computing aesthetics. In: de Oliveira, F.M. (ed.) SBIA 1998. LNCS (LNAI), vol. 1515, pp. 219–228. Springer, Heidelberg (1998)
10. Machado, P., Romero, J., Manaris, B.: Experiments in computational aesthetics: An iterative approach to stylistic change in evolutionary art. In: Romero, J., Machado, P. (eds.) The Art of Artificial Evolution: A Handbook on Evolutionary Art and Music, pp. 381–415. Springer, Heidelberg (2007)
11. Rigau, J., Feixas, M., Sbert, M.: Informational dialogue with van gogh's paintings. In: Eurographics Symposium on Computational Aesthetics in Graphics, Visualization and Imaging, pp. 115–122 (June 2008)
12. Romero, J., Machado, P., Carballal, A., Correia, J.: Computing aesthetics with image judgement systems. In: McCormack, J., do, M. (eds.) Computers and Creativity, pp. 295–322. Springer, Heidelberg (2012), http://dx.doi.org/10.1007/978-3-642-31727-9_11
13. Romero, J., Machado, P., Carballal, A., Osorio, O.: Aesthetic classification and sorting based on image compression. In: Chio, C.D., et al. (eds.) EvoApplications 2011, Part II. LNCS, vol. 6625, pp. 394–403. Springer, Heidelberg (2011)
14. Romero, J., Machado, P., Carballal, A., Santos, A.: Using complexity estimates in aesthetic image classification. Journal of Mathematics and the Arts 6(2-3), 125–136 (2012)
15. Romero, J., Machado, P., Santos, A., Cardoso, A.: On the development of critics in evolutionary computation artists. In: Raidl, G.R., et al. (eds.) EvoWorkshops 2003. LNCS, vol. 2611, pp. 559–569. Springer, Heidelberg (2003)

16. Ross, B.J., Ralph, W., Hai, Z.: Evolutionary image synthesis using a model of aesthetics. In: Yen, G.G., Lucas, S.M., Fogel, G., Kendall, G., Salomon, R., Zhang, B.T., Coello, C.A.C., Runarsson, T.P. (eds.) Proceedings of the 2006 IEEE Congress on Evolutionary Computation, July 16–21, pp. 1087–1094. IEEE Press, Vancouver (2006)
17. Santella, A., Agrawala, M., DeCarlo, D., Salesin, D., Cohen, M.: Gaze-based interaction for semi-automatic photo cropping. In: Proceedings of the SIGCHI Conference on Human Factors in Computing Systems, CHI 2006, pp. 771–780. ACM, New York (2006)
18. Suh, B., Ling, H., Bederson, B.B., Jacobs, D.W.: Automatic thumbnail cropping and its effectiveness. In: UIST, pp. 95–104. ACM (2003)
19. Wang, J., Cohen, M.F.: Simultaneous matting and compositing. In: Computer Society Conference on Computer Vision and Pattern Recognition (CVPR 2007). IEEE Computer Society (2007)
20. Zell, A., Mamier, G., Vogt, M., Mache, N., Hübner, R., Döring, S., Herrmann, K.U., Soyez, T., Schmalzl, M., Sommer, T., et al.: SNNS: Stuttgart Neural Network Simulator User Manual, version 4.2. Tech. Rep. 3/92, University of Stuttgart, Stuttgart (2003)
21. Zhang, M., Zhang, L., Sun, Y., Feng, L., Ma, W.Y.: Auto cropping for digital photographs. In: ICME, pp. 438–441 (2005)

Feature Construction Using Genetic Programming for Classification of Images by Aesthetic Value

Andrew Bishop[1], Vic Ciesielski[1], and Karen Trist[2]

[1] School of Computer Science and Information Technology
RMIT University, GPO Box 2476, Melbourne, Vic 3000, Australia
[2] School of Media and Communication
RMIT University, GPO Box 2476, Melbourne, Vic 3000, Australia
abishop@jetsystems.com.au, {vic.ciesielski,karen.trist}@rmit.edu.au

Abstract. Classification or rating of images according to their aesthetic quality has applications in areas such as image search, compression and photography. It requires the construction of features that are predictive of the aesthetic quality of an image. Constructing features manually for aesthetics prediction is challenging. We propose an approach to improve on manually designed features by constructing them using genetic programming and image processing operations implemented using OpenCV. We show that this approach can produce features that perform well. Classification accuracies of up to 81% on photographs and 92% on computationally generated images have been achieved. Both of these results significantly improve on existing manually designed features.

Keywords: Genetic Programming, Feature Construction, Image Aesthetics.

1 Introduction

Automatic classification or rating of images is a challenging task, but one with many applications, such as refining or sorting search results for images, automatically evaluating image compression settings or even providing real-time in-camera guidance to a photographer.

Automatic classification of an image according to its aesthetic value requires first analysing the image and producing 'features' or metrics that can be used to make a determination. We present a method of exploring those features automatically using Genetic Programming (GP). The programs are functions that operate on input images and produce a numeric result, which is used as a feature by a classifier.

Evolved programs will be tested on two datasets - photographs from dpchallenge.com and computer generated images created by an evolutionary art program (Figures 1 and 2).

We propose a method of evolving multiple feature construction programs sequentially. We will show that it is possible to evolve features that can out-perform manually constructed features by a significant margin.

J. Romero et al. (Eds.): EvoMUSART 2014, LNCS 8601, pp. 62–73, 2014.

Fig. 1. High rated (left) and low rated (right) photographs

Fig. 2. High rated (left) and low rated (right) evolved art

1.1 Goals

The main focus of our research is to determine whether genetic programming can create features that are useful for image aesthetics classification. In particular:

1. How can genetic programming be configured to evolve features that are useful for classification of images according to their aesthetic value?
2. Are the evolved features comparable to or better than manually devised features in terms of classification performance?
3. What distinguishing features of images are discovered by successful evolved programs?

2 Related Work

Our research uses genetic programming (GP) for feature construction in an image classification problem. We present here related work in those areas as well as previous work in computational aesthetics.

2.1 Genetic Programming for Image Classification

Zhang and Wong [8] used GP to classify images for medical diagnosis. They used a novel evolution strategy which simplified the programs while they were being evolved and showed improved performance over standard GP as well as neural networks, decision trees, naive bayes and nearest neighbour methods. Zhang and Ciesielski [7] used GP to find the locations of objects in images. They pre-computed a set of features of a sliding window over the input image. They showed improved performance on difficult detection problems compared to a neural network.

A limitation of these classification approaches is the reliance on a pre-defined feature set chosen prior to evolution of the genetic programs. The features are domain specific and as noted in [7], experiments with other feature sets showed improved performance in different situations.

Genetic Programming for Feature Construction. Feature construction is the creation of new attributes from an existing feature vector for the purposes of machine learning. GP is applicable to feature construction because of its flexibility in combining existing features [4].

Roberts and Claridge [6] used a co-evolutionary approach to solve object detection problems. They evolved feature construction and object detection programs simultaneously. They showed impressive performance on shape detection tasks and concluded that evolved features are more useful than human-designed ones. Krawiec and Bhanu [5] present an image recognition architecture using GP and cooperative co-evolution to evolve a set of feature construction programs. Their GP operators include OpenCV functions. They show good results on classification of radar images.

Image Aesthetics. Previous work in computational image aesthetics by Datta et al. [2] produced a set of 56 features for predicting whether a photograph was of high or low aesthetic value. They included global measurements of brightness and 'colourfulness', features influenced by photography composition techniques, wavelets for measurement of texture, size and ratio features, and some local features associated with regions of similar pixels. They used support vector machines and CART decision trees for evaluation and show around 70% accuracy on a two class problem of 'good' vs 'bad' photographs. Ke et al. [3] proposed similar features and achieved 72% classification accuracy on photographs from DPChallenge.com.

Ciesielski et al. [1] evaluated the features developed in [2] on photo.net photographs and a dataset of images generated by an evolutionary art program (Imagene). The generated images were rated by humans. They used several different classifiers combined with different feature selection methods and showed good performance on the Imagene dataset of up to 92% accuracy using a random forest classifier. They noted that the most important features for classifying Imagene images were related to global colour measurements.

We use the features developed by Datta et al. [2] for comparison with our evolved features, and also make a comparison with the work in [1].

3   Methodology

We use an iterative procedure to evolve feature construction programs. Firstly, a starting set of existing features is selected (this can be empty). The images are divided into training and test sets.

The evolutionary process proceeds as usual by creating an initial random population of programs from the available set of operators, and combining them using crossover and mutation to create new populations. Specifics of operators and fitness evaluation are described in Section 3.1. Fitness evaluation is performed indirectly using a decision tree classifier.

The evolutionary process runs for a fixed number of generations. Once finished, the most fit individual is obtained from the final population and is executed again over the set of training images to produce a feature value for each image. The resulting feature is permanently added to the set of existing features to be used by subsequent iterations.

The entire process is iterated and terminated manually once an acceptable level of classification accuracy is obtained. The result of this process is a sequentially constructed set of features with one new feature for each iteration. Once terminated, a decision tree is built from the final features of the training set. The classification accuracy of the decision tree on the withheld testing images is reported as the final accuracy of the set of evolved features.

3.1   Genetic Programming Configuration

The data types, terminals and operators used in the genetic programs are defined here. The output of a program is a single real-valued number which is the feature value for a particular image.

Data Types. There are three data types used in the genetic programs:

- *Floating point* Real valued floating point number.
- *Image* A two-dimensional matrix of floating point values. The image represents a single channel only, for example it may represent the brightness channel of an image or the result of an image operation.
- *Kernel* Represents a convolution kernel, a two-dimensional matrix of floating point values but of smaller dimensions than an image.

Terminals. Terminals for the GP program tree consist of image channels and random numbers.

- *Image Hue, Saturation, Brightness* These three channels are derived from the input image to the genetic program. The RGB source image is converted to HSL representation and the three separate channels are presented to the genetic program as separate terminals.
- *Random* A randomly generated value ranging from -10 to 10. This value remains constant for the program in which it is used.

Operators. Genetic programming operators are defined here. Image-processing operators are implemented using OpenCV functions.

- *Add, Subtract, Multiply, Divide* Standard arithmetic operators.
- *Mean, Stdev, Min, Max* These operators calculate statistics of the elements of an image matrix (OpenCV $meanStdDev()$, $minMaxLoc()$) .
- *Convolve* Performs a convolution of an input Image using an input Kernel. The resulting image has the same dimensions as the input image (OpenCV $filter2D()$).
- *Crop* This operation crops a region of an input image defined by four real valued inputs.
- *Kernel3x3* This operation creates a Kernel of dimension 3×3 from 9 input Floats.
- *AddScalar, MultiplyScalar* These operations take an input Image and add or multiply by a scalar value producing an Image result.
- *DownSample* This operation resizes an input Image to half its original dimensions (OpenCV $resize()$).
- *Threshold* Threshold calculates an output image by comparing each pixel in the input image to a threshold value. The resulting pixel in the output is set to 1 if it is greater than the threshold, otherwise 0 (OpenCV $threshold()$).
- *Sigmoid* This operation calculates the sigmoid or logistic value of the input Float.

Fitness Evaluation. Fitness of an individual is defined as the performance of a classifier on the training data set augmented by the feature calculated by the individual.

A training set consists of M example images, M class labels indicating either 'good' or 'bad' images, and a set of N previously calculated features forming an $M \times N$ matrix of real numbers.

The training set data is loaded at the beginning of the evolution process and each image is converted to a Hue-Saturation-Lightness representation.

To evaluate the fitness of an evolved program, the program is evaluated on each image in the training set by supplying the hue, saturation and lightness channels to the appropriate terminals in the program. After evaluation the program produces a real number for each image. This is the feature value.

This feature value is appended to the set of previously calculated features creating a new $M \times [N + 1]$ matrix. A CART decision tree classifier is trained on the new matrix and its classification accuracy assessed using 10-fold cross validation. The classification error rate is the fitness value of the evolved program (lower is better).

3.2   Data Sets

This work uses labelled data from two sources - computationally generated images and photographs from the DPChallenge web site. Each example image is rated by multiple people on a rating scale and the average of those ratings becomes the final image rating. The highest rated examples have been labelled 'good' and the lowest 'bad'.

Imagene. Imagene is a software application that generates images using genetic programming. It evolves functions that describe an image in terms of a mathematical formula.

The authors [1] of the dataset created 2260 evolved images and had them rated by 6 people on a scale of 1 to 7. Some examples are shown in Figure 2. For our research, the 450 highest rated and 450 lowest rated images were selected.

DPChallenge. dpchallenge.com is a web site that hosts photography challenge competitions. Competitions pose a topic and participants take a photograph that represents their interpretation. Some examples are shown in Figure 1.

The web site makes available the top 1000 and bottom 1000 rated images. These were collected and resized to be 320 pixels on their longest side, preserving their aspect ratio.

4   Experiments and Results

Here we describe the experiments used to evaluate the feature construction method. Section 4.2 details the experiment conducted on the evolved art dataset 'Imagene', the results achieved and an analysis of some of the evolved feature construction programs. The same results are given in section 4.3 for the DPChallenge photographic dataset. A discussion of some of the evolved features from an artistic viewpoint is given in Section 4.4.

4.1   Implementation

OpenCV v2.4 was used for image operations such as convolution, HSL conversion as well as providing the CART decision tree implementation for the fitness function. RMITGP v2.2 is used for the genetic programming framework. RMITGP is a software library developed by RMIT for Genetic Programming. It provides the algorithms for genetic program evolution.

4.2   Experiment with Imagene Evolved Art

An experiment was conducted on the Imagene dataset. The dataset of 900 labeled images was split into a training set (75%) and testing set (25%). The features developed in [2] were calculated for the entire dataset and were used for comparison.

The feature construction process was run for 38 iterations with each iteration having 50 generations of evolution (see Table 1). This resulted in 38 features.

Table 1. Evolution Parameters for Imagene Experiment

Population size	100	Depth at creation	4
Maximum Depth	12	Max Generations	50
Target Fitness	0	Mutation rate	0.28
Crossover rate	0.7	Elitism rate	0.02
Fitness	classification error	Number of images	674 train, 226 test
Size of images	500 x 500 pixels	Class distribution	450 good, 450 bad

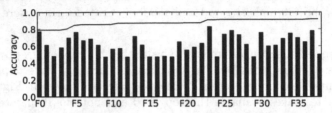

Bars show accuracy of individual features, line shows fitness value over iterations

Fig. 3. Imagene Experiment Individual Feature Accuracy

The classification accuracy using all evolved features is shown in Table 2. This accuracy figure is calculated by building a decision tree using the training set data and using it to predict the class labels for the test set. McNemar's test of correlated proportions is used as statistical test of the significance of differences in classification between the evolved features and the Datta features. There is a significant improvement over the Datta features with McNemar's test showing a p-value of < 0.05.

Table 2. Classification Accuracy on Imagene Dataset

Method	Accuracy	Precision	Recall	χ_1^2	p-value
Evolved	92.0%	0.92	0.93	5.92	0.015
Datta	85.0%	0.86	0.86		

Figure 3 shows the predictive accuracy of each feature on its own (bars) and the cumulative accuracy of all features (lines). The individual accuracies are calculated by creating a decision tree using the single feature and evaluating its performance on the test set. The cumulative accuracy is calculated by using all constructed features up to that point. The cumulative accuracy is also the fitness of the evolutionary process, which monotonically increases as the iterations progress. Large individual accuracies often coincide with an increase in the cumulative accuracy.

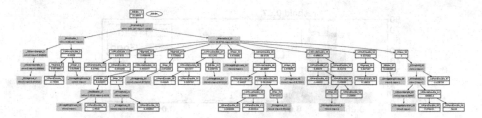

Fig. 4. Overview of Evolved Program for Imagene Feature F23

Analysis. Significantly improved classification results were achieved using the evolved features over the Datta features in this experiment.

Ciesielski et al. [1] performed experiments using Imagene images and the Datta features. Their experiments have been repeated on the dataset used here and a comparison is presented in Table 3. The four classifiers were tested with the feature selection method that gave the best result in [1], and also without feature selection. The evolved features show an improvement in all cases.

Table 3. Comparison with results using Datta features, with and without feature selection (FS)

		Evolved Features		Ciesielski et al.	
Classifier	FS Method	No FS	With FS	No FS	With FS
OneR	Sym	80.3%	80.3%	71.0%	71.0%
J48	Wrapper	89.7%	90.9%	86.9%	85.9%
Random Forest	CFS	91.8%	**92.9%**	**89.6%**	88.4%
SMO	Wrapper	89.9%	89.8%	86.5%	85.1%

Feature F23. An impression of the complexity of feature F23, the one found to be most important, can be had from Figure 4. It consists of 69 operations, of which 22 operations result in an image (the shaded nodes in the tree).

However the underlying operation is relatively simple to follow. The nodes on the left take the hue channel of the image, down-sample it twice shrinking the image dimensions by 1/4, and invert it. The majority of the nodes on the right side are related to the construction of a convolution kernel which simply shifts an image to the left by one pixel. The root node calculates the standard deviation of the convolved image which is the result of the program.

To summarize, the program essentially takes the standard deviation of the down-sampled hue channel of the image. This could be interpreted as a measurement of a 'high level structure' within the colors (hue) of the image. The down-sampled version essentially blurs the image, filtering out noise and fine detail and leaving behind higher level (lower frequency) structure.

70   A. Bishop, V. Ciesielski, and K. Trist

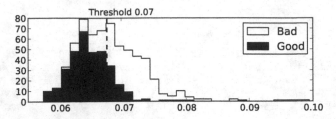

Fig. 5. Distribution of feature values for F37

Feature F37. This feature is more challenging to interpret. It could be described as the reciprocal of the maximum value of a convolution of the saturation channel. Good images predicted by this feature have high peak saturation values. This equates to 'strong colours' somewhere in the image. The distribution of image classes over the feature value is shown in Figure 5 and confirms that 'good' images have lower values using F37.

4.3 Experiment with Photographs

The same experiment was repeated for the DPChallenge dataset. The dataset of 2000 labelled images was split into 50% training and 50% test and the features developed in [2] were calculated for the entire dataset.

The feature construction process was run for 52 iterations each having 50 generations of evolution. This resulted in 52 features. The classification accuracy using all the features is shown in Table 4.

Table 4. Classification Accuracy on DPChallenge photographs

Method	Accuracy	Precision	Recall	χ_1^2	p-value
Evolved	80.9%	0.77	0.88	22.51	2.087e-06
Datta	72.5%	0.72	0.73		

Suprisingly, there was quite a large improvement over the Datta features to 80.9% compared to 72.5%. This is surprising because the Datta features were specifically designed for photographic aesthetics assessment.

The accuracy reported here using the Datta features is similar to the 70% reported in their work on photographs [2].

Analysis. The characteristics of some of the most important evolved features are discussed here. Importance is calculated from the decision tree construction process, with more important features typically used closer to the root of the tree.

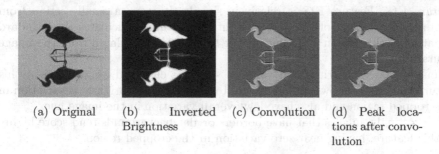

(a) Original   (b)   Inverted   (c) Convolution   (d) Peak loca-
                  Brightness   tions after convo-
                                                             lution

Fig. 6. Example operations for F41 on a 'Good' image

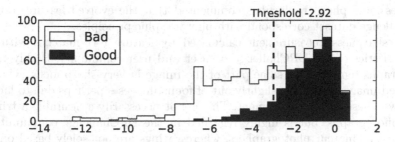

Fig. 7. Distribution of feature values for F41

Features F41 and F9. These features are the most important for classification and perform similar operations.

Feature F41 is quite surprising because on its own, it correctly classifies 80% of photographs in the DPChallenge dataset. Considering that, it is fairly simple in its operation. It could be described as a sharpness measurement.

The program inverts the brightness channel of the image, performs a convolution and returns the maximum value of the result. The evolved program has 42 operators, but most of them are unnecessary – although various operations are performed to construct the convolution kernel, its values remain more or less fixed. The convolution kernel works like an edge detector which emphasises sharp increases in brightness from left to right or bottom to top, and in particular corners where the lower-left values are darker than above or to the right.

An example of its operation is shown in Figure 6. The locations of the highest peaks of the convolution filter, typically located near 'corners' in the image, are shown in Figure 6(d).

Feature F9 is very similar to F41, but does not invert the image prior to applying the convolution. It is not clear why this would make a difference and why it survived evolution to contribute a significant amount to classification. One interpretation is that this feature simply adds another dimension to the measurement of sharpness. The convolution kernel in F9 is different to F41 and would emphasize sharpness in a different direction.

Feature F18. Feature F18 is relatively simple. It crops a small section from the upper left corner of the image brightness channel, calculates the standard deviation of this region and multiplies it by a factor calculated from the image saturation and hue.

Images above the threshold value of -0.2 are classified as good when this feature is used on its own. Good images tend to have low brightness variation in the cropped region and also have low overall variation in the image hue.

Interestingly, images that have borders or flat backgrounds tend score highly on this feature, having near zero variation in the cropped region.

4.4   Discussion

A professional photographer has commented that the evolved features on the DPChallenge dataset correspond with photographic principles.

The 'sharpness' measurement calculated by feature F41 matches with the characteristics of the DPChallenge dataset and user community. Highly rated photographs tend to have some part of the image in very sharp focus, whereas low rated images may have slightly out of focus images – perhaps due to lack of skill, awareness or poor equipment. This is not necessarily a desirable attribute of all photographs, but is highly regarded in the DPChallenge community of enthusiastic amateur photographers, where ratings are not solely based on the aesthetics or artistic value of the image, but also include technical considerations.

The photographer also noted that feature F18, that crops a region from the upper left of an image, fits with the compositional principle of foreground / background separation. This desirable attribute gives a three-dimensional quality to photographs by reducing background clutter and allowing the eye to focus on the subject of the photograph. Additionally, it is common to put the subject towards the lower-right in a photograph, leaving the upper-left with a plain background.

5   Conclusion

Our research has shown that genetic programming and image processing operations can be successfully combined to construct features for the purpose of image aesthetics classification. The evolved features have been compared to a set of manually created features and have been shown to improve classification accuracy by a statistically significant margin.

On the computer generated art dataset the evolved features improved classification accuracy to 92% from 85% for the manually created features.

On the photography dataset, a similar improvement was seen. The evolved features achieved 81% accuracy compared to 73% for manual features.

These results were somewhat unexpected. The intention at the beginning of this research was to evolve programs that could add useful features to existing manually designed ones. Instead, using genetic programming and a set of image processing operations, evolution produced features that perform better than those developed manually through careful consideration and research.

The most surprising example of the success of these experiments is that a single feature on the photography dataset achieved an 80% classification accuracy (see Section 4.3), where manually designed features achieved 73%.

For photographs, features relating to sharpness and image brightness were highly predictive. Also noteworthy is an interesting feature that simply considered the variation in brightness of the upper left corner of an image. In the case of the computer generated images, features representing colour and structure were the most discriminative.

We believe that the approach presented here is promising and warrants further investigation. Other datasets of art should be tested to see if this method can evolve features predictive of aesthetics, or if the features evolved here can generalise to other datasets (e.g. paintings). This method may also be applicable generally to image classification tasks.

References

1. Ciesielski, V., Barile, P., Trist, K.: Finding image features associated with high aesthetic value by machine learning. In: Machado, P., McDermott, J., Carballal, A. (eds.) EvoMUSART 2013. LNCS, vol. 7834, pp. 47–58. Springer, Heidelberg (2013)
2. Datta, R., Joshi, D., Li, J., Wang, J.Z.: Studying aesthetics in photographic images using a computational approach. In: Leonardis, A., Bischof, H., Pinz, A. (eds.) ECCV 2006. LNCS, vol. 3953, pp. 288–301. Springer, Heidelberg (2006)
3. Ke, Y., Tang, X., Jing, F.: The design of high-level features for photo quality assessment. In: Fitzgibbon, A., Taylor, C.J., LeCun, Y. (eds.) CVPR (1), pp. 419–426. IEEE Computer Society (2006)
4. Krawiec, K.: Genetic programming-based construction of features for machine learning and knowledge discovery tasks. Genetic Programming and Evolvable Machines 3(4), 329–343 (2002)
5. Krawiec, K., Bhanu, B.: Coevolution and linear genetic programming for visual learning. In: Cantú-Paz, E., et al. (eds.) GECCO 2003. LNCS, vol. 2723, pp. 332–343. Springer, Heidelberg (2003)
6. Roberts, M.E., Claridge, E.: Cooperative coevolution of image feature construction and object detection. In: Yao, X., et al. (eds.) PPSN 2004. LNCS, vol. 3242, pp. 902–911. Springer, Heidelberg (2004)
7. Zhang, M., Ciesielski, V.: Genetic programming for multiple class object detection. In: Foo, N.Y. (ed.) AI 1999. LNCS, vol. 1747, pp. 180–192. Springer, Heidelberg (1999)
8. Zhang, M., Wong, P.: Genetic programming for medical classification: a program simplification approach. Genetic Programming and Evolvable Machines 9(3), 229–255 (2008)

Authorship and Aesthetics Experiments: Comparison of Results between Human and Computational Systems

Luz Castro, Rebeca Perez, Antonino Santos, and Adrian Carballal

Department of Information and Communication Technologies
University of A Coruña, A Coruña, Spain
{maria.luz.castro,rebeca.perezf,nino,adrian.carballal}@udc.es

Abstract. This paper presents the results of two experiments comparing the functioning of a computational system and a group of humans when performing tasks related to art and aesthetics. The first experiment consists of the identification of a painting, while the second one uses the Maitland Graves's aesthetic appreciation test. The proposed system employs a series of metrics based on complexity estimators and low level features. These metrics feed a learning system using neural networks. The computational approach achieves similar results to those achieved by humans, thus suggesting that the system captures some of the artistic style and aesthetics features which are relevant to the experiments performed.

1 Introduction

Art may be considered to be innate to human beings. We have learnt to use our bodies and the tools around us from the beginning of recorded history, not just to communicate but also to express our artistic motivations.

The development of computing has inevitably led to the pursuit of generating systems which are capable, not just of supporting artists, but also of complementing them. Ada Lovelace, the daughter of the famous poet Lord Byron and arguably the first programmer in History, forecast in her writings the possibility of creating computers with artistic capabilities.

However, creating computer systems which can automatically perform artistic tasks is a complex and often controversial field. Even the definition of concepts such as art, beauty and aesthetics generate complex debates in areas such as Philosophy and Art Psychology. Moreover, making art has always been subject to a considerable subjective element where individuals and the emotional and social environments surrounding them have a direct impact.

In spite of these difficulties, there are several researchers who explore the creation of computational systems related to art and aesthetics. Some experiments aim at the achievement of systems which are capable of classifying and evaluating images without needing an interaction with users [6].

Following this line, it is necessary to have a component capable of "perceiving" a work of art and performing its classification/ordering/evaluation. In other

J. Romero et al. (Eds.): EvoMUSART 2014, LNCS 8601, pp. 74–84, 2014.
© Springer-Verlag Berlin Heidelberg 2014

words, this component would carry out the image classification or ordering according to some aesthetic or artistic features. There are a great number of papers presenting experiments related to these types of systems. We should highlight the special issue of the Journal of Mathematics and the Arts [4], and some previous papers at this conference, as well as in other fields [1,5,8]. This system would possess a great application by itself when integrated in search engines, as a pedagogical application or as support to artistic researchers all over the world.

From our point of view, creating these systems is hugely relevant within the framework of research into computational aesthetics. This paper compares an artificial system and those of human beings with different artistic training. For this purpose, two tests were performed, based on the validation methodology presented in [12]: one consisting of identifying the authorship of works by three different painters and another one based on aesthetic evaluation and appreciation by means of the psychological test developed by Maitland Graves. Both, the results of comparing humans and a computational system and the worth of the proposed metrics may be significant in this context.

2 Experiments Involving Humans

This section presents the experimental design of both tests with humans.

2.1 Authorship Experiments

How can humans acknowledge the authorship of a painting? What kind of features, colors or shapes should it have in order to be classified within the author's own style? What makes us say, when faced with a work of art; this is a "Mondrian" or a "Van Gogh"?

In order to start the experiment, we consider style as a system of shapes with significant qualities and expression through which the artist's personality becomes visible, as well as the perspective of a group framed in time. A given style consists mainly of a series of elements of form and motives interconnected by the so called "artist's expression". Nevertheless, the very creator of works of art is submitted to a huge subjective and contextual criterion which makes their work vary through time. Thus, although their characteristics remain constant, their works may be framed within several periods, touching upon different styles. This can be seen, for example, in the different works by Van Gogh, from the cool hues and realism of "The Potato Eaters" from 1885 to, for instance, the famous and well known "Starry Night" from 1889 (Figure 1). Those people who are not experts in art may well identify both works as belonging to two different authors, showing the great relevance of a well trained CAA for these types of problems.

For this reason, for the purpose of this experiment it was decided that we would work with paintings by Picasso, Kandinsky and Monet. The three of them show in their works paintings from different styles and periods which make their identification difficult. Nevertheless, they are recognizable enough by the general public so that they constitute a sound basis.

(a) The Potato Eaters (Realism)   (b) The Starry Night (Postimpressionism)

Fig. 1. Example of paintings belonging to the same author (Van Gogh) but framed in different periods

A total of 666 images by the already mentioned artists were selected, form various stages and styles, taken from the Internet, and distributed as follows: 212 images of Picasso works, 339 by Monet and 115 by Kandinsky. The experiment was carried out under controlled conditions within the University of A Coruña. Sixty-two humans took part, most of them university students between the ages of 18 and 25 (28 females and 34 males). Each subject was requested to evaluate a total of 30 works randomly chosen and distributed equally among the three authors. A high number of evaluations allow the elimination of false positives and avoiding the possibility of only evaluating the most recognizable works by the authors by chance, thus biasing results.

Every work was treated before the experiment in order to eliminate any kind of seal or signature by the author which would give hints to the subjects. Moreover, an application was designed covering the whole display on computers without Internet connection, so that each user was monitored and their answers recorded and processed through a binary code.

Subjects were handed a reference book acting as previous training before the performance of the identification test. The book contains 27 images by each author and an identifier ("A","B","C") instead of their names. These images were also anonymous. Subjects were constantly monitored in order to stop them from using support material and no external aid was provided.

Subjects were asked to answer a series of questions about themselves so as to allow a bias based on their sex, age and artistic experience, so as to compare if there is any difference in the percentage of right answers among the group with some kind of experience in the art field (to be called from now on "Art1") and those who did not ("Art0").

Next, an application displays randomly and subsequently each of the 30 images in the group. The user must only mark the type he/she considers that the work belongs to (Type A corresponds to Kandinsky, Type B to Monet and Type C to Picasso) and then click on the "next" button. Based on previous studies showing that the time during which the image is displayed does not influence aesthetic preference significantly, no maximum time limit was set. Users know at all times how many images they have evaluated and how many are left, however, they are not allowed to return at any time. At the end of the test, they are shown the achieved result.

2.2 Aesthetics Appreciation

The second experiment is focused on Maitland Graves' psychological test. This test yields the capacity for acknowledging some basic principles of aesthetic nature defined by the author; such as unity, predominance, balance among elements, variety, continuity, symmetry, proportion and rhythm.

Users in our experiment were provided with a short description of the test goal and the procedure to be followed. Thus, each individual was shown 30 items comprising two or three designs which were similar to each other (Figure 2). These 30 designs were randomly selected from the 90 in the test. In each item, one of the designs corresponds to the already mentioned criteria, thus being a correct image, while the other one (or the other two) do not comply with one or more of these principles.

The average percentage of correct answers resulting from answering randomly to the test is 48.3%, due to the fact that some of the items were made up of three images.

In addition to the original work of Graves, which shows an average percentage of correct answers of 49.4, there are different works that show the results obtained with this test on different samples of humans [3]. Eysenck and Castle [2] obtained a 64.4% success in populations with artistic knowledge. The Portuguese Institute for Employment and Vocational Training [9] obtained a 61.87% success in the case of students of Fine Art degrees vs random Portuguese individuals.

Also there are studies in which instead of human populations have been using mathematical and computational models [9]. In this case, Romero et al. obtained a success rate of 64.9% using a heuristic approach and a 71.67% through artificial neural networks.

3   Developed System

The developed system is based on a feature extractor and a neural network.

The feature extractor shown in [9] has been available. The extractor is based on low level metrics, edge detection filters and complexity estimators inspired by [7]. To start with, the extractor standardizes images to a format of 128 x 128 pixels in order to avoid the different relations between width and height, thus facilitating the extraction process. Later on, the image is divided into three channels: hue, saturation and value (HSV). Four families of metrics are then extracted from the image: metrics based on compression error, Fractal Dimension based on Zipf distribution and statistics (mean and typical deviation).

In compression-based metrics, the ratio between the error generated by a compression method and the compression ratio is calculated (this calculation is made

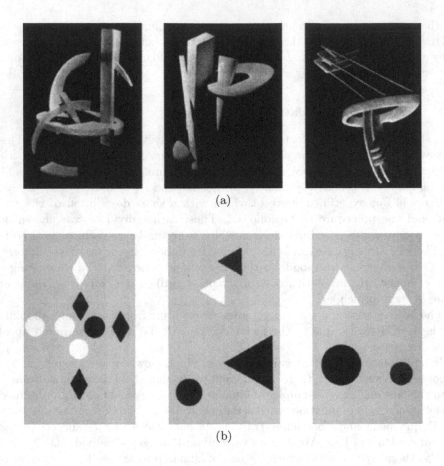

(a)

(b)

Fig. 2. Examples of images from the psychological test where humans tend to choose the wrong image

for JPEG and fractal compression, with three compression ratios in each case). Those metrics based on Zipf's Law use two values per channel, corresponding to the slope value and the correlation with the slope of the Zipf distribution of the value of the image pixels. For the value channel, the extractor also determines the Fractal Dimension of the original image and of the same one, after having applied three different types of Sobel filters. These filters allow a more accurate vision and identification of the image edges by approaching the gradient according to the image intensity. The Fractal Dimension was measured by means of using a similar technique to the one used by Taylor et al. [13], consisting of a simple method in which the image is turned into black and white, while the Fractal Dimension is estimated by means of the "box-counting" technique. This method allows cutting the image into small "boxes" and analyzing each one of them separately so as to obtain more satisfactory results. A Sobel filter was used in order to obtain the Fractal Dimension of the edges. Later on, the Fractal Dimension of the resulting image was calculated in total.

With the purpose of determining the variation of the features which are inherent to the painting, the image was divided into five equally-sized regions: four squares and one big rectangle overlapped in the center. Later on, the metrics of each partition are calculated.

Using each of these sub-images provides information about features which are as relevant as symmetry and balance. This process entails a total of 246 measurements. The neural network is a backpropagation MLP with 246 neurons in the input layer, 12 in the hidden one and 3 in the output layer. Thirty independent repeats were carried out during the training phase for each of the neural networks with the goal of achieving statistically significant results. Training, test and validation sets were randomly created for each repeat, containing 70%, 10% and 20% of the patterns, which were later on accurately applied to each of the different architectures in the neural networks. The training of the neural networks ends when any of these criteria is met: 1500 training cycles or an average quadratic error in the training and test phases lower than 0.005. These parameters and the topology were empirically established in previous experiments of different research groups [10,11].

In the aesthetic evaluation experiment, there were a very small number of patterns, which entailed the risk that the results were scarcely significant if the choice of training sets was not the right one. Therefore, a technique named on 20-fold cross-validation was carried out, which, in this case, yielded satisfactory results. Patterns were randomly distributed in 20 independent sets with a similar size among them (18 of them contain 5 patterns and two of them contain 4 patterns). Out of these 20 independent sets, 19 were used for the training, while only one of them was used for the test. Thus, none of the test patterns was included during the training, thus guaranteeing that the result has not been biased by a previous training. This process was repeated 20 times for every set, so that the results obtained comprise every possible case. An average of all the results obtained in each one of the sets is performed. The metrics corresponding to the Value channel of the image are used in this experiment (60 in total).

4 Results: Authorship Test

For the authorship identification experiment of the three selected artists (Monet, Picasso and Kandinsky), the percentage of right answers was 81.82%. Tests were made with different combinations of metrics in order to evaluate their relevance. Figure 1 shows the results of the two best combinations of features and of the human groups. Net1 corresponds to all the metrics (246) and Net2 is similar to Net1 but without sub-images (41 metrics). A network trained with the metrics based on compression and those of mean and statistical deviation achieved a 78% rate of correct answers.

Kandinsky's images are those achieving the best classification, with a practically zero error percentage, while Picasso's images are the ones which get the

Table 1. Comparison of the results obtained by the human groups (Art0 and Art1) and the neural networks (Net1 and Net2) identifying authorship

Approach	Description	Accuracy
Art0	38 individuals without art knowledge	83.42%
Art1	24 individuals with art knowledge	85.36%
Net1	264 metrics using all sub-images and all HSV channels	81.82%
Net2	41 metrics not using sub-images and using all HSV channel	78.00%

smallest percentage of right answers. These errors are usually found in paintings from styles or periods which are atypical in the painter, very distant from their best known works. For example, an observer could mistake the authorship of several Picasso works and those by Monet because of the treatment of form and color, as shown in Figure 3.

(a) Gabriele Münter Painting in Kallmünz (1903)

(b) In The Forest (1904)

Fig. 3. Examples of images by Kandinsky which observers tended to catalogue as either Monet's (a) or Picasso's (b)

As regards the experiment involving humans, the 62 individuals examined were divided into two sets: those who claimed not to possess any previous artistic experience (39 of them) (Art0) and those who claimed to have some artistic knowledge (23) (Art1).

The total rate of right answers is 84.43%. However, the rate of right answers in the group with some artistic experience is higher than that of the sample without any previous knowledge (85.36% vs. 83.42%). The images with the highest number of errors may be seen in Figure 4, 93.1% of errors (Fig. 4a) and 78.05% (Fig. 4b). Both are images by Kandinsky, attributed to Monet. The error percentage of Kandisnky's images is 71%, while the percentages in Picasso's and Monet's are around 90%.

(a) Doora Maar's portrait (1937)   (b) Crucifixion (1930)

Fig. 4. Examples of works which got the worst results in both neural networks authorship identification experiments

5   Results: Aesthetic Validation Test

The aesthetic validation tests carried out consisted of Maitland Graves' psychological test: 90 items with the goal of identifying the best image from an aesthetic point of view. For this purpose, the ANN is simultaneously provided with metrics from both images.

The first architecture used with the ANN consists of 120 neurons (corresponding to the 60 features extracted from the Value channel of each image) in the input layer, 5 in the hidden layer, and 2 in the output layer. Its percentage of right answers was 66.33%.

With the aim of improving its evaluation and checking the importance of the metrics in the results elaboration, only 20 out of the 60 metrics proposed by the extractor were used in the next experiment: those corresponding to the full image and to the rectangle superimposed at the center. Efficiency improved significantly, moving from a percentage of right answers of 66.33% to 70.41%.

The overall results from the 62 individuals correspond to only 46.2% of right answers, although those individuals with some previous artistic experience yielded better scores (42.56% vs. 52.32%). Table 2 shows a graph of the percentage of right answers by humans and computational systems. Systems A and B correspond to neural architectures 120-5-2 and 40-5-2.

Table 2. Comparison of the results obtained by human groups (Art0 and Art1) and neural networks (Net1 and Net2) in the aesthetic validation psychological test

Approach	Description	Accuracy
Art0	38 individuals without art knowledge	42.56%
Art1	24 individuals with art knowledge	52.32%
Net1	60 metrics using all sub-images and Channel V	66.33%
Net2	20 metrics using one sub-image and Channel V	70.41%

6   Conclusions

The results of the comparison between a computational system with respect to a set of humans in carrying out tasks related to the art and aesthetics have shown as the system is able to recognize the studied paintings similarly to humans. In addition, the system also seems to be able to identify different aesthetic principles such as those used in the DJT better than the human population evaluated.

In the research, a computational system based on Artificial Neural Networks has been used with low-level metrics related to complexity, Fractal Dimension, Zipf, as well as typical deviation, average and the three color channels integrating the HSV (hue, saturation and luminosity). The experiment was carried out in two stages: one for identifying the authorship of a series of paintings and a validation test of aesthetic evaluation. Its performance has been compared with the results obtained by a set of 62 human, mostly university students.

Monet, Kandinsky and Picasso were chosen as painters to be classified for the authorship test, due to the wide dissemination of their works and the differences between their pictorial periods. The total number of works comprised 666 images by the painters (212 by Picasso, 339 by Monet and 115 by Kandinsky). Participants were asked to classify 30 random images into three main groups: Type "A", "B" and "C", each of them related to its author. They were not allowed to use any reference material, although they had been previously shown 27 images of each type, without providing any information about their authorship. The results achieved by humans have an average of right answers of 84.43%, while those of the system achieved 81.82%. By using only compression error based metrics, together with the average and typical deviation, the result achieved is 78%. This result suggests that these metrics are the most significant ones in the proposed set.

Maitland Graves' "Design Judgement Test" was employed for the aesthetic evaluation tests. This consists of showing two or three images to the subject and asking him/her to indicate which one is the most correct. Only one of the images in the set complies with aesthetic composition criteria perfectly well, while the others do not comply with some of those principles. The results achieved by humans are 52.32% in the best-case scenario, vs. 74.49% by the system.

Nevertheless, it should be pointed out that the data is not comparable. The network has been previously trained with a set of images from the test itself, while participants in the experiment did not have any previous knowledge of it. Of course, it may be inferred that there is some degree of aesthetic sensitivity in human beings guiding them in their aesthetic judgement. However, this sensitivity should not always follow the principles defined by Maitland Graves in his test.

Anyhow, it may be deduced from the experiment results that the system, using just some metrics extracted from the image, has been capable of applying correctly some of the aesthetic principles defined by Maitland Graves in his test.

It may also be inferred that some of the metrics (or metric combinations) are capable of extracting or identifying the existence or inexistence of some of these principles.

Finally, the system has yielded similar results to those by humans in the authorship identification task from images. This suggests that the metrics used (specifically, those related to compression) allow a differentiation between different "styles" characteristic of each author, with results similar to those achieved by an average human being.

This work combines and compares the results of aesthetic appreciation from two different perspectives, the computational and the human, showing that in some cases the first might provide better results.

Acknowledgments. This research was partially funded by: Spanish Ministry for Science and Technology, research project TIN-2008-06562/TIN; Xunta de Galicia, research project XUGA-PGIDIT-10TIC105008PR.

References

1. Ekárt, A., Joó, A., Sharma, D., Chalakov, S.: Modelling the underlying principles of human aesthetic preference in evolutionary art. Journal of Mathematics and the Arts 6(2-3), 107–124 (2012)
2. Eysenck, H.J., Castle, M.: Comparative study of artists and nonartists on the maitland graves design judgment test. Journal of Applied Psychology 55(4), 389–392 (1971)
3. Götz, K., Götz, K.: The maitland graves design judgement test judged by 22. Perceptual and Motor Skills 39, 261–262 (1974)
4. Greenfield, G., Machado, P.: Special issue: Mathematical models used in aesthetic evaluation. Journal of Mathematics and the Arts 6(2-3) (2012)
5. den Heijer, E.: Evolving glitch art. In: Machado, P., McDermott, J., Carballal, A. (eds.) EvoMUSART 2013. LNCS, vol. 7834, pp. 109–120. Springer, Heidelberg (2013)

6. Lewis, M.: Evolutionary visual art and design. In: Romero, J., Machado, P. (eds.) The Art of Artificial Evolution, pp. 3–37. Springer, Heidelberg (2008)
7. Machado, P., Cardoso, A.: Computing aesthetics. In: de Oliveira, F.M. (ed.) SBIA 1998. LNCS (LNAI), vol. 1515, pp. 219–228. Springer, Heidelberg (1998)
8. Li, Y., Hu, C., Minku, L., Zuo, H.: Learning aesthetic judgements in evolutionary art systems. Genetic Programming and Evolvable Machines 14(3), 315–337 (2013), http://dx.doi.org/10.1007/s10710-013-9188-7
9. Machado, P., Romero, J., Manaris, B.: Experiments in computational aesthetics. In: Romero, J., Machado, P. (eds.) The Art of Artificial Evolution: A Handbook on Evolutionary Art and Music, pp. 381–415. Springer, Heidelberg (2007)
10. Romero, J., Machado, P., Carballal, A., Osorio, O.: Aesthetic classification and sorting based on image compression. In: Chio, C.D., et al. (eds.) EvoApplications 2011, Part II. LNCS, vol. 6625, pp. 394–403. Springer, Heidelberg (2011)
11. Romero, J., Machado, P., Carballal, A., Santos, A.: Using complexity estimates in aesthetic image classification. Journal of Mathematics and the Arts 6(2-3), 125–136 (2012)
12. Romero, J., Machado, P., Santos, A., Cardoso, A.: On the development of critics in evolutionary computation artists. In: Raidl, G.R., et al. (eds.) EvoWorkshops 2003. LNCS, vol. 2611, pp. 559–569. Springer, Heidelberg (2003)
13. Taylor, R.P., Micolich, A.P., Jonas, D.: Fractal analysis of Pollock's drip paintings. Nature 399, 422 (1999)

An Indirect Fitness Scheme
for Automated Evolution of Aesthetic Images

Gary Greenfield

University of Richmond, Richmond, VA 23173, USA
ggreenfi@richmond.edu
http://www.mathcs.richmond.edu/~ggreenfi/

Abstract. Recently, the question of whether artifacts obtained from a generative art system can be judged as creative based on the characteristics of their offspring has received considerable attention. Here, we focus on the question of whether aesthetic images can be evolved by considering characteristics of their offspring. We introduce a formal model for designing fitness functions for use in automated evolution of aesthetic images whereby genotypes are evaluated relative to certain characteristics of their offspring. We describe the results of an experiment using such an indirect fitness scheme that promotes offspring diversity in order to help select for parent phenotypes with desired symmetry and complexity properties. We use as our image generation platform a variant of the Sims' classical *Evolving Expressions* generative art system.

1 Introduction

In the study of computational *creativity* [3,29] the problem of understanding the role "novelty" plays is fundamental, whereas in the study of computational *aesthetics* [4,5,16,18,28] the problem of evaluating art works on the basis of their aesthetic merit is of primary interest. This latter problem has been identified as one of the more difficult open problems in evolutionary music and art [30]. Recently, Kowaliw et al. [23,24] and Dorin and Kolb [8] have explored various definitions of creative novelty, and their consequences, within the context of generative art by employing what we would term indirect indicators. The platforms they used were Dawkins well-known line drawing system *Biomorphs* [7] and a texture generation system called *EvoEco*. Inspired by their ideas, we propose a new scheme for designing fitness functions for evaluating aesthetics within generative art. We use as our platform a variant of the Sims' classical *Evolving Expressions* generative art system [31].

When discussing evolutionary art systems, it is important to distinguish between those adopting interactive evolution based on human-in-the-loop mechanisms to guide evolution [10,31,37] versus those adopting fully automated evolution where explicit pre-defined fitness functions guide evolution [12,22,27,36]. Although it can be argued that the "mix and match" use of interactive and automated evolution has been extant since the inception of evolutionary art (see Baluja et al. [1] or Sprott [32–35]), over time the terms "interactive evolution"

J. Romero et al. (Eds.): EvoMUSART 2014, LNCS 8601, pp. 85–94, 2014.

and "automated evolution" have become even further blurred thanks to the use of hybrid techniques ranging all the way from evolving fitness functions [6], to adaptive fitness functions [26], to multiple fitness functions and the use of multi-objective optimization [13, 19], to fitness functions which serve as user tools to be integrated into interactive evolution [9, 24]. However, to be clear, in this paper we will only consider explicitly defined fitness functions for fully automated evolution. Evolutionary computation in this context is often referred to as "genetic learning" [14] because genotypes are trained over time to yield phenotypes obeying certain rigid criteria.

Dorin and Kolb [8] make elaborate claims for the imagery capable of being produced by *Biomorphs*. In our experience, line drawing generative art systems — compare, for example Bentley [2] — bias towards centered compositions. On the other hand, color-based texture systems such as *EvoEco* usually make it difficult to evaluate the imagery evolved due to color biases i.e., color confounds composition. *EvoEco* is also peculiar because its uses GP trees to generate color components, uses local color information as the key inputs, has a limited set of primitives with which to compute, and permits only very small trees. For these, and other reasons we turn to a gray scale tree-based generative art texture system which uses the "method of evolving expressions" first introduced by Sims [31].

This paper is organized as follows. In section two we review some recent computational creativity research. In section three we develop our fitness function. In section four we give the details of our evolutionary set-up and present our results. Section five provides a different slant to the work and section six contains our formal model and conclusion.

2   On the Role of Novelty

Although it is neither easy to come to grips with, nor easy to get a handle on, the underlying theme of the empirical work by Kowaliw et al. [23, 24] on defining and analyzing creative novelty associated with an artifact obtained using a generative art system rests primarily on the notion of considering the characteristics of a small number of offspring of the artifact that are generated wholly by mutation. This motivation and theory behind this approach is further developed by Dorin and Korb [8].

Using the line drawing generative art system *Biomorphs* [7], Kowaliw et al. [23] compare a set of randomly generated images against a set of images generated using interactive evolution and a set of images evolved using a creativity metric. They conclude that randomly generated *Biomorphs* are the least creative and their evolved *Biomorphs* are the most creative. To arrive at this conclusion, they partition the image space of all 200×200 pixel *Biomorphs* on the basis of a set of representatives whose feature vectors — vectors whose six components are statistically based image processing measurements that include three geometric moments, an edge-area measurement, a histogram-related entropy measurement, and a homogeneity measurement — have the property that most *Biomorphs* will have feature vectors that are close to one of them. This set of representatives establishes the "world view" of image space. Now, by isolating pairs of feature vector components, the idea is to measure the creativity of a *Biomorph* by considering how k of its mutated offspring are situated with respect to values of the pair of components provided by the world view. Automated evolution thus selects for *Biomorphs* whose offspring are most dissonant from the world view.

Using the agent-based pixel-coloring generative art system *EvoEco*, Kowaliw et al. [24] next use the concept of pre-computing a set of representatives constituting a world view in order to enhance re-populating the next generation in an interactive evolutionary art system that evolves *EvoEco* images. That is, the interactive system can be configured so that re-population occurs either by presenting to the user random genomes, genomes chosen in accordance with the creativity metric mentioned above, or genomes chosen for "phenotype distance" attributes. User studies are then conducted to study the efficacy of, and preferences for, the various options.

Rather than focus on the question of whether evolved images are creative as determined by the characteristics of their offspring, we want to focus instead on the question of whether aesthetic images can be evolved by considering characteristics of their offspring. This idea of exploration based on differences is reminiscent of a scheme proposed by Johnson [21] to identify individuals in a GA population-based algorithm that have useful unrecognized structures: "take individuals, apply a hypermutation to them (i.e. a mutation at many times the normal rate) several times, and see which produced the most novel solutions, then use those as parents for the next generation." One suggestion investigated by Johnson for implementing this [20] is "giving parents a score of one for each novel child and then assigning the child the sum of its parents' scores."

3 Our Fitness Function

To leverage the idea that an image can be evaluated on the basis of what it's offspring portend, as each new image (i.e., genotype) p arises for consideration — either as a member of the initial population or by resulting from recombination followed by mutation — nine offspring or child genotypes $o_1, \ldots, o_9$ are assigned to it. In our GP based system, these offspring are obtained solely by mutating p so that, independently, with probability 0.05, each node of p is replaced by a new node of the same arity.

Our objective is to reward genotypes that promote offspring diversity in hopes of selecting for image phenotypes exhibiting texture variety and texture complexity. The key component of our fitness evaluation rests upon a measure of the difference between two images, in this case offspring and parent. Previously, it has been demonstrated that when using the method of evolving expressions, differences between two images in small subregions can be indicators of an overall image difference [11]. Therefore, rather than incorporating computationally expensive global measurements involving factors such as compressibility, brightness, or symmetry we can try to exploit this local-global principle by measuring the difference between two images using only a small number of 10×10 pixel subregions. Here, we use four such subregions, symmetrically located with respect to the center. They are located at the four corners of our 100×100 pixel phenotype images. Thus only $(4 \times 100)/(100 \times 100)$ or 4% of each image is used to determine the difference measure. If corresponding pixels between the two images of these subregions give gray scale values that are more than 0.25 apart in absolute value, then one difference point is awarded. Given two 100×100 pixel gray scale images A and B, this implies that the measure of their difference, $m_D(A, B)$, will lie between 0 and 400.

Although summing this difference measure using a parent and its child over all nine of the parents' offspring is consistent with the novelty measurement approach found in Lehman and Stanley [25], preliminary experiments revealed that automated evolution could defeat its intent simply by evolving a genotype whose phenotype had a nearly solid intermediate color. Part of the problem is due to the naive definition of $m_D(A, B)$ of course, and in retrospect, the emergence of solid opaque phenotypes makes sense because no additional rewards for the aesthetic attributes of the parent itself are being incorporated into the fitness calculation. To remedy this oversight, after summing the difference measure between parent and mutated offspring over the nine offspring, we then scale this quantity by two factors: one promoting contrast within the phenotype of the parent, $m_C(p)$, and the other promoting both symmetry and contrast within the phenotype of the parent, $m_S(p)$. In this way, we arrive at the fitness value $f(p)$ for the genotype p defined by:

$$f(p) = m_S(p) \cdot m_C(p) \cdot \Sigma_i m_D(p, o_i).$$

To measure combined contrast and symmetry for a 100×100 pixel image I, we again exploit the local-global principle and use the four 10×10 subregions located at the corners. For each grouping of four pixels — one from each subregion — chosen so they they are symmetric with respect to vertical and horizontal reflection through the center, we first average their expression tree values to obtain v. We now consider only those groups where each of the contributing pixels is within 0.05 of v. We set l equal to the number of such groups where $v < 0.3$ and h equal to the number of such groups where $v > 0.7$. Finally, we let $m_S(I) = l + h - |l - h|$. Clearly this quantity is non-negative. If all 100 groups of four pixels contribute to the calculation, and if exactly half the resulting v's are above 0.7 and half are below 0.3 then the maximum value of 100 for this measure will be obtained. To evaluate contrast alone we use the *central* 10×10 subregion of the image I, and set a equal to the number of pixels that yield a value above 0.75, b equal to the number of pixels that yield a value below 0.25, and let $m_c(I) = a + b - |a - b|$. Using a similar analysis, it follows that this measure also lies between 0 and 100, whence we see that our image fitness value $f(p)$ must lie in the range from 0 to $(100)(100)(9)(400) = 36,000,000$.

4   Evolved Images

The variant of Sims' evolving expressions method we use has its antecedents in a gray scale image generation system developed by Greenfield [17]. Images are formed from genomes (expression trees) by evaluating the trees at the pixel coordinates and then interpreting the outputs as colors. Thus expression trees can be viewed as bottom-up image processing networks. In our GP system, the internal nodes of the genotype can be either unary functions or binary functions and the terminals must be either variables or constants assuming values between zero and one. The set of building block functions, or *primitives*, for the internal nodes was designed so that inputs and outputs all lie between zero and one. This makes it easy to map outputs to the typical linear 8-bit gray scale ramp consisting of 256 colors ranging from black to white. The system uses 5 unary primitives, 15 binary primitives and one thousand constants (0.000, 0.001, ..., 0.999). Details appear in Greenfield [15]. It should be noted that this generative system is resolution independent, which means that by scaling them, pixel coordinates used as inputs are normalized to decimal values between zero and one, so an image with any desired dimensions can be rendered. However, since here our focus is on investigating new metrics for aesthetics, all images will be rendered as 100×100 pixel thumbnails.

For our evolutionary runs, we enforced the restriction on genotypes that the number of nodes always lie between 75 and 150. Our population size was 50. The initial, or generation zero, population was randomly generated. Thereafter, to obtain the next generation the top 16 individuals were preserved, and 17 pairs were used to repopulate as follows: two distinct genomes were drawn from the pool of survivors; those two genomes were crossed using subtree crossover; and the two resulting genomes were then mutated as described previously. The evolutionary run lasted for 1500 generations. Thus fitness was calculated for $50 + (1500)(34) = 51,150$ genomes.

To examine the results of automated evolution, after every 100 generations the highest rated individual together with its 9 offspring were preserved, and at the conclusion of the run a 10×15 matrix of images was output with the 15 preserved parents appearing sequentially in the top row and their nine offspring appearing in the columns beneath them. This visualization scheme for encapsulating an entire evolutionary run is similar to one first proposed by Greenfield [17]. Figure 1 shows the results from a sample run.

What is immediately apparent from Figure 1 is that even when parent phenotypes look similar, the sets of offspring that were used to evaluate their fitness can look radically different. Of course this is easily explained by the fact that similar parent phenotypes arising from functionally equivalent similar parent genotypes will have multiple opportunities to achieve high fitness as various sets of mutated offspring are generated and evaluated. This coupled with the fact that we use elitism eventually identifies those parents that gave rise to maximally divergent sets of offspring. One benefit is that there is no need to try and identify and remove from consideration redundant offspring; evolution solves this problem for us.

The fact that similar parent phenotypes can persist for hundreds of generations is demonstrated by the output from the run shown in Figure 2. It shows two phenotypes that "rule" the population for long periods of time. Figure 2 also

Fig. 1. A sample 10×15 output matrix showing the individuals of highest ranked fitness at generations 100, 200, ..., 1500 along the top row and their nine mutated offspring used during their fitness calculation in the column directly beneath them

highlights the fact that our fitness function favors parent genotypes whose phenotypes have strong black and white contrast. Recall that this attribute was only examined at the center of the parent phenotype and, at least sometimes, at the four corners of the parent phenotype, so it is gratifying to see its presence throughout the images. This preference for strong contrast in the parent was chosen so that it facilitates comparison between the composition style one identifies with *Biomorphs* versus some of the many composition styles that are associated with the method of evolving expressions using our set of primitives.

Figure 1 and Figure 2 also remind us that we selected for symmetry in the parent, and it is gratifying to see its eventual emergence in both cases. On the other hand, the output shown in Figure 3 shows that persistence of parental phenotypes is not the same as stagnation because now one can detect minor changes in the dominant phenotype over time. Johnson remarked about the difficulty of comparing the novelty resulting from his parent-child novelty scheme with a random scheme [20]. We do not know how to design a test that would measure either the efficiency or effectiveness of using offspring to help evaluate fitness (i.e., to convincingly compare what would happen if we simply omitted the summation term that relies on the m_D parent-offspring comparison measurements), but experience suggests to us that if it were not present evolution would "lock on" to a local maximum genotype fairly quickly, one that would not

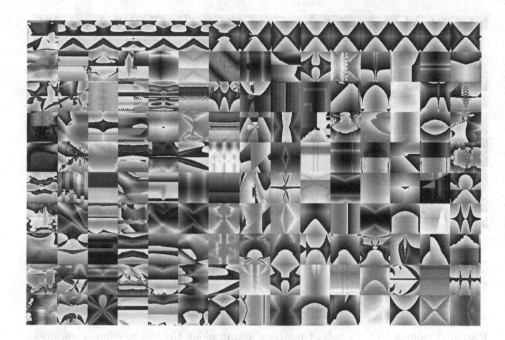

Fig. 2. A sample 10×15 output matrix revealinging along the top row two phenotypes that persist for hundreds of generations as the most fit individuals in the population

be so easily replaced. In other words, the fact that fitness is dependent upon the set of offspring can work to our advantage in that a small change in parent genotype coupled with a fresh set of offspring can offer greater opportunity to dislodge the current most fit individual.

5   Diversity or Plasticity?

Our motivation was that we were trying to incorporate a measure of offspring diversity into our fitness calculation. But perhaps the argument can be made that we are not evolving genotypes exhibiting offspring diversity but rather we are evolving genotypes exhibiting parental plasticity. By this we mean the parent phenotype has very unstable genetic characteristics such that with very high provability even a single point mutation in the parent genotype would result in a drastic (catastrophic? lethal?) change in the phenotype. It could be an indication of a population with the property that surviving individuals are highly fit but nearly all their offspring would perish. We are unaware of what the artificial life implications might be for simulated evolution in a wider context subject to this kind of evolutionary pressure.

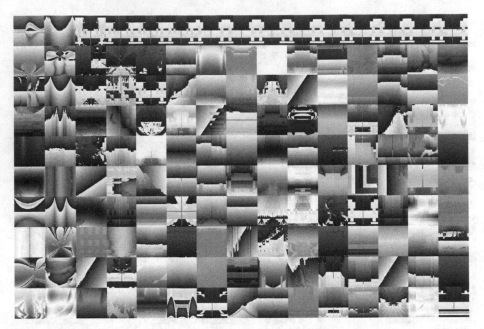

Fig. 3. A sample 10×15 output matrix showing along the top row minor variation occurring within a persistent, dominant phenotype over time

6   Conclusion

Our one-off experiment incorporating the characteristics of mutated offspring into an aesthetic evaluation of a parent is but one instantiation of a fitness function arising from a more general fitness function design model: Given parent p and mutated offspring $o_1, \ldots, o_k$ fitness takes the form

$$f(p) = m_P(p) \cdot \Sigma_i m_R(p, o_i)$$

where the measurement m_P of p is intrinsic to p, and the measurement m_R of p is relative to its offspring o_i. In this paper we did not employ very sophisticated techniques when designing either m_P or m_R. Our instantiation was straightforward and naive. We believe interesting results can be achieved using other choices for m_P and m_R. Moreover, our design framework is suggestive of an even broader class of fitness function models which we also feel are worth exploring. For example, one could also introduce terms for considering characteristics of the offspring relative to each other.

References

1. Baluja, S., Pomerleau, D., Jochem, T.: Towards automated artificial evolution for computer-generated images. Connection Science 6, 325–354 (1994)
2. Bentley, K.: Exploring aesthetic pattern formation. In: Soddu, C. (ed.) Generative Arts Conference Proceedings, pp. 201–213 (2002)

3. Bentley, P., Corne, D.: Creative Evolutionary Systems. Academic Press, Waltham (2002)
4. Birkhoff, G.: Aesthetic Measure. Harvard University Press, Cambridge (1933)
5. Blackwell, A., Dodgson, N.: Computational aesthetics as a a negotiated boundary. Leonardo 43(1), 88–89 (2010)
6. Colton, S.: Automatic invention of fitness functions with application to scene generation. In: Giacobini, M., et al. (eds.) EvoWorkshops 2008. LNCS, vol. 4974, pp. 381–391. Springer, Heidelberg (2008)
7. Dawkins, R.: The evolution of evolvability. In: Langton, C. (ed.) Artificial Life, pp. 201–220. Addison-Wesley, Reading (1989)
8. Dorin, A., Kolb, K.: Creativity refined: bypassing the gatekeepers of approriatness and value. In: McCormack, J., d'Inverno, M. (eds.) Computers and Creativity, pp. 339–360. Springer (2012)
9. Ekárt, A., Joó, A., Sharma, D., Chalakov, S.: Modeling the underlying principles of human aesthetic preference in evolutionary art. J. Math. and the Arts 6(2-3), 107–124 (2012)
10. Graf, J., Banzhaf, W.: Interactive evolution of images. In: McDonnell, J., et al. (eds.) Genetic Programming IV: Proceedings of the Fourth Annual Conference on Evolutionary Programming, pp. 53–65. MIT Press (1995)
11. Greenfield, G.: Art and artificial life — a coevolutionary approach. In: Bedau, M., et al. (eds.) Artificial Life VII Conference Proceedings, pp. 529–536. MIT Press, Cambridge (2000)
12. Greenfield, G.: Designing metrics for the purpose of aesthetically evaluating images. In: Purgathofer, W., et al. (eds.) Computational Aesthetics 2005, Eurographics Workshop on Computational Aesthetics in Graphics, Visualization and Imaging, pp. 151–158. Eurographics Association (2005)
13. Greenfield, G.: Evolving aesthetic images using multiobjective optimization. In: Sarker, R., et al. (eds.) Proceedings of the 2003 Congress on Evolutionary Computation, IEEE Press, Canberra (1909)
14. Greenfield, G.: Genetic learning for biologically inspired aesthetic processes. International Journal on Artificial Intelligence Tools 15(4), 577–598 (2006)
15. Greenfield, G.: Mathematical building blocks for evolving expressions. In: Sarhangi, R. (ed.) 2000 Bridges Conference Proceedings, pp. 61–70. Central Plain Book Manufacturing, Winfield (2000)
16. Greenfield, G.: On the origins of the term computational aesthetics. In: Neumann, L., et al. (eds.) Computational Aesthetics 2005, pp. 9–12. Eurographics Association, ACM Press, New York (2005)
17. Greenfield, G.: Tilings of sequences of co-evolved images. In: Raidl, G.R., et al. (eds.) EvoWorkshops 2004. LNCS, vol. 3005, pp. 427–436. Springer, Heidelberg (2004)
18. Greenfield, G., Machado, P.: Guest editors' introduction, Special Issue: Mathematical Models used in Aesthetic Evaluation. J. Math. and the Arts 6(2-3), 59–64 (2012)
19. den Heijer, E., Eiben, A.E.: Evolving art using multiple aesthetic measures. In: Di Chio, C., et al. (eds.) EvoApplications 2011, Part II. LNCS, vol. 6625, pp. 234–243. Springer, Heidelberg (2011)
20. Johnson, C.: Finding diverse examples using genetic algorithms. In: John, R., Birkenhead, R. (eds.) Developments in Soft Computing. Advances in Soft Computing, pp. 92–99. Physica/Springer-Verlag (2001)
21. Johnson, C.: Understanding complex systems through examples: A framework for qualitative example finding. Systems Research and Information Systems 10(3-4), 239–267 (2001)

22. Jones, M., Agah, A.: Evolution of digital images. IEEE Transactions on Systems, Man, and Cybernetics 12(3), 261–271 (2002)
23. Kowaliw, T., Dorin, A., McCormack, J.: An empirical exploration of a definition of creative novelty for generative art. In: Korb, K., Randall, M., Hendtlass, T. (eds.) ACAL 2009. LNCS, vol. 5865, pp. 1–10. Springer, Heidelberg (2009)
24. Kowaliw, T., Dorin, A., McCormack, J.: Promoting creative design in interactive evolutionary computation. IEEE Transactions on Evolutionary Computation 16(4), 523–536 (2012)
25. Lehman, J., Stanley, K.: Beyond open-endedness: quantifying impressiveness. In: Adami, C., et al. (eds.) Proceedings of the Thirteenth International Conference on Artificial Life (ALIFE XIII). MIT Press (2012)
26. Machado, P., Romero, J., Santos, M.L., Cardoso, A., Manaris, B.: Adaptive critics for evolutionary artists. In: Raidl, G.R., et al. (eds.) EvoWorkshops 2004. LNCS, vol. 3005, pp. 437–446. Springer, Heidelberg (2004)
27. Machado, P., Cardoso, A.: All the truth about NEvAr. Artifical Intelligence 16, 101–118 (2002)
28. Machado, P., Romero, J., Manaris, B.: Experiments in computational aesthetics: an iterative approach to stylistic change in evolutionary art. In: Romero, J., Machado, P. (eds.) The Art of Artificial Evolution: A Handbook on Evolutionary Art and Music, pp. 381–415. Spinger, Berlin (2008)
29. McCormack, J., d'Inverno, M.: Computers and Creativity. Springer, Berlin (1992)
30. McCormack, J.: Open problems in evolutionary music and art. In: Rothlauf, F., et al. (eds.) EvoWorkshops 2005. LNCS, vol. 3449, pp. 428–436. Springer, Heidelberg (2005)
31. Sims, K.: Artificial evolution for computer graphics. In: Proceedings SIGGRAPH 1991, vol. 25, pp. 319–328. ACM Press, New York (1991)
32. Sprott, J.: Automatic generation of general quadratic map basins. Computers & Graphics 19(2), 309–313 (1995)
33. Sprott, J.: Automatic generation of iterated function systems. Computers & Graphics 18(3), 417–425 (1994)
34. Sprott, J.: Automatic generation of strange attractors. Computers & Graphics 17(3), 325–332 (1993)
35. Sprott, J.: The computer artist and art critic. In: Pickover, C. (ed.) Fractal Horizons, pp. 77–115. St. Martin's Press, New York (1996)
36. Staudek, T.: Computer-aided aesthetic evaluation of visual patterns. In: Barrallo, J., et al. (eds.) ISAMA-Bridges 2003 Conference Proceedings, University of Granada, Granada, Spain, pp. 143–150 (2003)
37. Todd, S., Latham, W.: Evolutionary Art and Computers. Academic Press, London (1992)

A Novelty Search and Power-Law-Based Genetic Algorithm for Exploring Harmonic Spaces in J.S. Bach Chorales

Bill Manaris[1], David Johnson[1], and Yiorgos Vassilandonakis[2]

[1] Computer Science Department, College of Charleston,
66 George Street, Charleston, SC 29424, USA
manarisb@cofc.edu, dsjohnso1@g.cofc.edu
[2] Music Department, College of Charleston,
66 George Street, Charleston, SC 29424, USA
vassilandonakisy@cofc.edu

Abstract. We present a novel, real-time system, called Harmonic Navigator, for exploring the harmonic space in J.S. Bach Chorales. This corpus-based environment explores trajectories through harmonic space. It supports visual exploration and navigation of harmonic transition probabilities through interactive gesture control. These probabilities are computed from musical corpora (in MIDI format). Herein we utilize the 371 J.S. Bach Chorales of the Riemenschneider edition. Our system utilizes a hybrid novelty search approach combined with power-law metrics for evaluating fitness of individuals, as a search termination criterion. We explore how novelty search can aid in the discovery of new harmonic progressions through this space as represented by a Markov model capturing probabilities of transitions between harmonies. Our results demonstrate that the 371 Bach Chorale harmonic space is rich with novel aesthetic possibilities, possibilities that the grand master himself never realized.

Keywords: Novelty Search, Genetic Algorithm, Markov Model, Harmony, Generative Music.

1 Introduction

Harmonic Navigator (the Navigator, for short) is the latest system from a multi-year interdisciplinary effort exploring artificial intelligence techniques in analysis, composition, and performance of musical works. It is an interactive platform for exploring the harmonic space of distinct or composite musical styles (controlled by the musical corpora loaded into the system). It may be used to compose new harmonic sequences, as well as to support real-time performance by dynamically generating music in collaboration with human performers. The target audience for the Navigator includes composers and performers with basic musical training (minimally, first year music theory at the university level).

J. Romero et al. (Eds.): EvoMUSART 2014, LNCS 8601, pp. 95–106, 2014.
© Springer-Verlag Berlin Heidelberg 2014

The Navigator generates harmonic sequences through interactive user control. It combines a GUI visualization of harmonic possibilities (i.e., how typical it is for certain harmonies to appear next in a given harmonic sequence), and real-time, gesture-based user input (see Fig. 1). The system is initialized using a particular, stylistically appropriate corpus of music, from which the system extracts harmonies and learns harmonic transition probabilities. Herein, we utilize the Riemenschneider collection of 371 J.S. Bach Chorales. We also have access to the Classical Music Archives 14,000+ MIDI corpus, along with a few additional smaller corpora, for further experimentation.

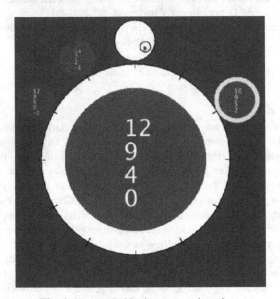

Fig. 1. Harmonic Navigator user interface

The Navigator combines Markov models, genetic algorithms, novelty search, and power-law metrics. In particular, the Markov models are used to learn harmonic transitions. A genetic algorithm (GA) is used to suggest interesting possibilities as the user navigates the harmonic space. The GA is guided using the novelty search approach. Finally, power-law based metrics are used to assess the aesthetic value of generated individuals (harmonic progressions) according to some predetermined target piece (e.g., one of the Bach chorales, or something totally different stylistically, e.g., Led Zeppelin's "Stairway to Heaven"). While the Novelty Search algorithm is encouraging creation of novel individuals, the power-law metrics are used to determine if enough individuals have been generated that meet some basic aesthetic criteria, to be used as the termination condition.

The architecture of the Navigator consists of two main services, a harmonic generator and a gesture engine (see Fig. 2). The gesture engine ensures that an implemented gestural device supports the required user tasks as explained below in the User Interface section. The harmonic generator provides the user interface with all services necessary to generate harmonic flows via the GA and the Markov Model.

The paper is organized as follows: Section 2 discusses background research and related projects, Section 3 focuses on how we extract and represent harmonic data, as well as alternate musical corpora that may be used for training, and Section 4 describes the user interface. It focuses on the visual representation of the harmonic space and the transition possibilities available. The next two sections describe how we combine Markov models and genetic algorithms to search for interesting harmonic sequences. Finally, we present closing remarks and ideas for future work.

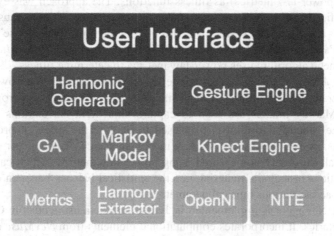

Fig. 2. Harmonic Navigator architecture using a Microsoft Kinect

2   Background

Within the last 50 years there have been numerous applications of computing and artificial intelligence in analysis, generation, composition, and performance of music.

Experiments in Music Intelligence (EMI) is the most comprehensive work in auto-mated computer music generation to-date [1]. EMI performs feature analysis on a corpus of musical works and uses results from this analysis to train Markov models. Using these models, EMI can then automatically compose pieces in a style similar to the corpus, arguably some better than others. EMI works off-line and has been used to generate numerous pieces in the style of various composers.

The *Corpus-Based Harmonic Progressions Generator* [2] mixes stochastic selec-tion via Markov models and user influence to generate harmonic progressions in real time. The user enters information to specify harmonic complexity and tension, as well as a bass-line contour. This is used by the system to influence the selection of harmo-nies from the trained Markov models, and to generate a harmonic progression.

Continuator is an interactive music performance system which accepts musical in-put from a human performer. It completes musical material in the same style as the user input [11]. Using a musical corpus, the system trains several Markov models (of various orders), structured in decreasing order of information retrained. Human performer input is matched against the various Markov models starting with the most informed one, and continuing (by reducing the length of the user input) until a match is found. The corresponding Markov model is used to generate a musical continuation. This makes the system sometimes generate perfect reproductions of earlier musical input, and other times less accurate repetitions (introducing interesting variations).

NEvMuse [6] is an experiment in using genetic programming to evolve music pieces based on examples of desirable pieces. *NEvMuse* uses artificial music critics (employing power-law metrics) as fitness functions. The approach was evaluated by training artificial neural networks to predict the popularity of 2000 musical pieces with 90.70% accuracy. The system was used to autonomously "compose" variations of J.S. Bach's Invention #13 in A minor (BWV 784). Similarly to *NevMuse*, the Navigator's genetic algorithm uses power-law metrics to determine fitness.

Monterey Mirror [7] uses Markov models, genetic algorithms and power-law metrics to generate musical phrases in real-time, based on musical input from a human performer. Markov models are used to capture short-term correlations in melodic material. The genetic algorithm is then used to explore the space of probable note combinations, as captured by the Markov model, in search of novel, yet similar melodic material. Similarity is measured using power-law metrics, which capture long-term correlations in melodic material, i.e., the statistical balance between expectation and surprise across various musical parameters [5, 10].

Harmonic Navigator is implemented in Jython and Java using custom GUI, MIDI, and OSC libraries. It incorporates computational elements from *NevMuse* and *Monterey Mirror* to allow human performers to navigate the space of musical harmonies using a gesture-based interface. Different aspects of this system have been presented elsewhere. The corpus-based approach with an emphasis on music analysis, composition, and performance is presented in [8]. The user interface aspects of the system appear in [9]. Herein we focus on the evolutionary aspects on the system.

3　Data Representation

From a music theory standpoint, harmony has played a key role in formal construction and narrative in both tonal and non-tonal systems. Furthermore, harmonic context not only defines musical texture by contextualizing lines (melodies) and creating consonance/dissonance hierarchy, but also, across time, it outlines formal trajectories, controls pacing and phrasing, as well as levels of tension and release. Well-established pitch systems have strong harmonic syntax, which dictates how strongly or loosely vertical sonorities (chords) can be connected in sequence. This syntax in some styles (e.g., common practice functional tonality) is as strong as in natural language, with chords assigned specific functions (much like nouns being subjects or objects in a phrase), hierarchy, weight and even punctuation. Thus, a musical phrase may close with a cadence (a codified chord sequence), "the basis of all Western musical form starting with Gregorian chant" [12]. Within such a pitch system, the listener is guided and can orient themselves by the harmonic flow, which also sets up expectations for what is to follow and how long a specific phrase will be. Of course, this opens the door for introducing surprises, such as deceptive cadences (e.g., V-vi), mode mixture derived harmonies, or modulations to new tonal centers [13].

In this context, the Navigator allows a user who is familiar with the musical style at hand to meaningfully interact with upcoming harmonies, selecting chords that have strong probability of connecting well to the existing sequence of chords (i.e., the harmonic sequence context), or possibly go to unexpected harmonic places. Additionally, we provide a GA process for generating harmonic recommendations based on novelty search and power-law metrics (as described below).

3.1 Musical Corpora

We are currently using the 371 MIDI pieces of the Riemenschneider collection of Bach chorales. Additionally, we have access to the Classical Music Archives (CMA) corpus, which consists of 14,695 classical MIDI encoded pieces. This corpus is augmented with 500+ MIDI pieces from other music genres including Jazz, Rock, Country, and Pop (a total of approximately 15,600 music pieces), for additional experimentation.

Stylistic integrity is paramount when selecting pieces to be used with the Navigator. For instance, combining 12-tone pieces with Renaissance pieces would most likely create a harmonic space with two disjoint subspaces. This is undesirable, if not pointless. On the other hand, combining, say, modal Jazz with impressionist pieces (e.g., Debussy) might create a somewhat coherent harmonic space, which may be interesting to investigate and navigate.

3.2 Harmony Extraction

Harmony extraction is a difficult problem even in MIDI musical corpora. Since our task is statistical in nature (i.e., we calculate probabilities of harmonic transitions), we try to simplify and normalize the information at hand.

For each MIDI piece, we calculate the average note duration across the whole piece and set a duration threshold to remove notes that are too short in duration to be part of structural harmonic voicings (e.g., ornamental pitches such as passing or neighbor tones). This is a parameter that can be set by the user, during training of the system, and is experimentally determined based on the musical style.

Next, we normalize melodic phrases by converting the MIDI pitch data into a standard representation that independent of musical key. To do so, we calculate the key of the piece by creating a histogram of pitch-durations. We assume the most frequent pitch class (total durations) is the key (regardless of octave).[1] Next, from the various instances of the pitch class across octaves (e.g., C3, C4, C5),[2] we select the most frequent one (e.g., C4) and set it as the *base tone* (i.e., canonical pitch 0). All other

---

[1] Even for pieces with modulations, the pitch class with the longest accumulated duration (across the piece) defines the tonic center of that piece.

[2] C4 represents the pitch C in the 4th octave (i.e., MIDI pitch 60).

pitches (MIDI numbers) in the piece are replaced by the difference between their MIDI pitch number and the MIDI pitch number of the base tone. For example, if a piece begins with C4, D4, B3 (and assuming C4 is the base tone), it is converted to 0, 2, -1.

Then we extract harmonies. For our purposes, a harmonic interval is any interval between two notes that overlap in time.

3.3   Harmony Representation

For each harmonic interval, we store $(i_1, i_2, ..., i_n)$, where i represents the interval from the piece's base tone. For example, consider the following two harmonies from a piece with base tone C4:

> **Harmony 1:** (C3, C4, E4, G4, B4)
> **Harmony 2:** (D4, FS4, A4, CS5)[3]

Using the above process, these harmonies would be represented as:

> **Harmony 1:** (-12, 0, 4, 7, 11)
> **Harmony 2:** (2, 6, 9, 13)

where the first number, -12, represents the root of the first harmony (C4), which has -12 distance from the piece's base tone. The other four numbers, (0, 4, 7, 11), are the corresponding pitch distances (intervals) from the piece's base tone. This representation is complete, i.e., it can represent all harmonies (even dissonant ones), and is consistent with music theory. The advantage of this representation is that it defines an aesthetically-relevant notion of harmonic distance across chords. Also, it allows us to define interval-based Zipf metrics for use in the fitness function of our genetic algorithm (discussed later).

4   User Interface Design

The Harmonic Navigator interface presents available harmonies as a dynamic navigable space. It offers two primary modes of interaction: a gesture-based harmonic transition selector, called the *harmonic palette*, and a harmonic-flow scrubber, which presents a global view of a flow being generated. The first UI provides a tree-level view, and thus allows for localized control and inter-harmony navigation (see Fig. 1). The second UI provides a forest-level view, and supports scrubbing and editing actions. Both views use colors to indicate harmonic density (or tension) calculated using Legname's density degree theory [3]. This approach measures the complexity of a

---

[3] FS4 is the pitch F sharp, 4th octave (i.e., MIDI pitch 66).

harmonic interval's sine wave representation to estimate the consonance/dissonance of the harmonic interval.

Similarly to Monterey Mirror, the genetic algorithm runs continuously (in the background) to suggest interesting harmonic flows. A special bright ring around a follow-up harmony signifies that this is the harmony recommended by the genetic algorithm. Since the genetic algorithm is running continuously, it is possible for the recommended harmony to change (if the genetic algorithm discovers a better choice), while the user is contemplating. As the user navigates forward (or backward) through the harmonic space, the genetic algorithm restarts from this particular point in the space looking for aesthetic recommendations on how the current harmonic flow may be completed. Again, the user has a choice - they may accept the recommendation or ignore it. Either way, the genetic algorithm adapts and continues in parallel with the user's navigation through the space.

The system's user interface is described in more detail elsewhere [9]. Demos of the system's user interface include:

- a demo of using the Harmonic Palette interface via a Microsoft Kinect to control navigation; and
- a demo of the Harmonic Flow interface for scrubbing GA generated harmonic progressions.

These are available at http://www.cs.cofc.edu/~manaris/navigator .

5   Markov Model

Harmonic Navigator uses Markov models to construct an n-dimensional matrix of how often one subsequence of harmonies resolves into a given harmony. Once trained, the system can be used (via the gesture interface) to generate various harmonic sequences (or harmonic flows) that are derived from the training corpus.

It is possible for the system to recreate an exact training sequence (i.e., recreate the harmonies in a musical piece used for training). This is more probable for smaller training sets, as a Markov model would mostly memorize separate (disconnected, independent) sequences. However, as the training set grows and introduces ambiguity (i.e., training sequences overlap across different places), generating exact training sequences becomes exponentially improbable. This is where the power of the Navigator lies, i.e., to facilitate exploration and discovery of novel harmonic flows that are probabilistically plausible (at least, at a local level) and are stylistically consistent with the training corpus. Given our reliance on power-law metrics for fitness, we have observed that Markov orders of 1, 2 or 3 work well with this approach. Higher orders may result in memorization of harmonic sequences, and thus reduce the potential for discovery of novel harmonic ideas.

6   Evolutionary Algorithm

To guide users through the harmonic space, the Navigator utilizes a hybrid Novelty Search and power–law based genetic algorithm. Novelty Search is used to guide the

GA through the space while a power-law based fitness function is used to store the elite individuals and terminate the search.

The size of our corpora generates a large harmonic space with nearly endless possibilities to explore. The fitness function may also incorporate a melodic contour, as in [2] to provide a high-level structure and impose melodic constraints to the exploration. In this case, harmonies are chosen by the GA based on how well they fit the provided contour in addition to the power-law based metrics. Using a melodic contour helps prune the space for more efficient navigation. In cases of smaller corpora, where there may not be enough harmonic material, using a melodic contour may be too restrictive.

It should be noted that these GA-generated flows are not necessarily the most probable ones (i.e., as would be produced by the Markov model). However, the flows are consistent with the Markov model, i.e., they are built only of harmonic transitions found in the training corpus.

6.1   Power-Law Metrics

During the last decade, our group has explored Zipf's law and other power laws in music information retrieval, computational aesthetics, and artificial creativity (see http://sger.cs.cofc.edu). Due to limited space, here we provide an overview of power-law metrics and cite earlier publications.

Power laws are statistical models of proportions found in natural and artificial phenomena. Human language, music and brain waves are a few such phenomena.

Zipf's law is one of many power laws. It corresponds to phenomena (e.g., language in books), where the probability, $P(f)$, of a certain event occuring (e.g. a word in a book) is proportional to its frequency of occurrence, f, as follows:

$$P(f) = 1/f \tag{1}$$

For instance, if the most frequent word in a book (e.g., "a") appears x times (say, ~1000 times), the 2nd most frequent word appears $x/2$ times (~500 times); the 3rd most frequent word appears $x/3$ times (~333 times); the 4th appears $4/x$ times (~250 times); and so on.

We have found that music exhibits power-law proportions across many dimensions, including pitch, duration, harmonic intervals, and distance of repeated notes, among others. Evaluation experiments indicate that power-law proportions (measured across many dimensions per musical piece) correlate with human aesthetics (i.e., aspects of how this piece is perceived by humans) [5, 6, 10]. In particular, we have used power-law metrics to classify musical pieces with high accuracy, in terms of composer, style, and pleasantness, among other possibilities.

For the harmonic navigation task, we have developed three new power-law metrics:

- **Chord Metric** - calculates the power-law proportions of chords across a harmonic flow.

- **Chord Distance Metric** - first, measures the distance of identical chords across a harmonic flow; then, calculates the power-law proportions of those distances.
- **Density Degree Metric** - first, calculates the density degrees of chords across a harmonic flow; then, calculates the power-law proportions of those density degrees.[4]

As stated earlier, our approach combines Markov models and power-law metrics. Markov models capture shorter-term correlations. Power-law metrics capture longer-term correlations, and overall balance in harmonic flow structure. The combination of the two techniques (i.e., Markov models to provide raw genetic material, and power-law metrics for fitness) allows to effectively search the harmonic space for flows (chord progressions) which make aesthetic sense both at the tree level (e.g., voice leading) and at the forest level (harmonic development).

6.2   Genotype Representation

The genetic population is initialized randomly through the Markov model. Each genotype represents a particular harmonic flow (a sequence of chord choices).

Throughout evolution, genotypes always remain consistent with the Markov model (i.e., there is a set of valid transitions in the Markov model which can generate a given genotype). Therefore, the crossover and mutation operations must maintain this consistency. In essence, the GA explores the space of all harmonic transitions captured by the Markov model, in search of the best possible harmonic flows (genotypes).

- The **mutation operator** randomly selects a point in the genotype and replaces the remainder with a partial flow generated from the Markov model.
- The **crossover operator** randomly selects a pivot point (a common harmonic subsequence) in two individuals (parents). Then, it cross-swaps the subsequences before and after the pivot. The length of the pivot subsequence is consistent with the Markov order. (If not such pivot point exists, the parents are deemed incompatible, and they do not produce offspring.)

To decide which genotypes survive, we calculate a novelty value of each genotype (see section 6.3), as well as, a more traditional fitness value (see section 6.4).

6.3   Novelty Search

Novelty search is used to guide the GA through the possible paths of the harmonic space. Rather than using a standard objective-based fitness function, which may constrain search results by moving towards local maxima, novelty search rewards individuals with new behavior. This helps to open up the search and visit places that an objective based search would not have otherwise [4].

---

[4] For more information on constructing such metrics, see [11].

To implement novelty search within an existing GA, the objective based fitness value is replaced by a novelty value. This novelty value is higher for genotypes that are further away from (a) the rest of population, and (b) an archive of previously found novel genotypes. The archive ensures the path of the search does not return to previously visited spaces.

Within our system, the novelty of an individual (harmonic flow) is measured as follows. First, we calculate the behavior of the generated harmonic flow. To do so, we construct a vector consisting of the density degrees of all harmonies in the flow. Next, we average the distance (mean squared error) between the individual's vector and those of the k-nearest neighbors of the population, where k is a constant determined via experimentation. The greater the average distance, the sparser of a region the individual resides in, hence a more novel individual.

If the average distance of the individual meets a specified threshold (also determined via experimentation) it is considered *novel* and is added to the archive. The most novel individuals of each population are used to reproduce the population.

6.4   Melody Guided Fitness

While the novelty metric (described in the previous section) is used to decide which individuals survive during evolution, we use an objective-based fitness measurement to decide, during evolution, which individuals to output to the user. Also, we use this measurement to decide when to terminate the search. So, in essence, we "piggyback" on the novelty search as it explores the harmonic space for novel harmonic flows, and we observe. Any novel harmonic flow that passes the objective-based fitness test, we save.

The objective-based fitness utilizes a target piece, which is provided by the user as input to the Navigator. The target piece is used as an example of balance and aesthetics we would like to emulate. It is possible to provide a set of target pieces. Objective fitness is calculated by comparing the distance (mean squared error, or MSE) between the power-law metrics of an individual and the corresponding metrics of the target.

Next, we determine how well the genotype fits the input melody. This is done as follows:

- we juxtapose the individual to the melodic contour;
- we calculate the density degrees of the harmonies in the individual;
- we add the normalized pitch values from the melody to each corresponding harmony in the individual; and
- we calculate the density degrees of the new harmonies.

The density degrees of the new progression are then compared to the original density degrees by calculating the distance (MSE) between the two vectors. A progression that closely fits the melodic contour will have a small MSE because adding the melody pitch to each harmony of the progression will have a small effect on the harmonic density.

For example, if the melody's pitch is already contained within the harmony then the density degree will not change (the MSE will be zero). But, if the addition of the melody's pitch generates a tense harmony, then the density degree is much higher (a larger MSE).

Adding the weighted MSE values of each measurement generates the final fitness value. As the GA is running (using Novelty Search to reproduce), the fitness value is used **only** to determine which progressions to save. If an individual exceeds a given objective-based fitness threshold, it is saved, while the GA continues searching. The GA terminates after enough individuals have been saved, or after a max number of generations.

Additional results, generated music, and demos of the Navigator's user interface are available at http://www.cs.cofc.edu/~manaris/navigator .

7   Conclusion and Future Work

We have presented the Harmonic Navigator, an interactive system for exploring harmonic spaces of distinct (or composite) musical styles, and for dynamically generating music in collaboration with human performers. The Navigator uses a genetic algorithm to help guide users through the space, while allowing them to have control by providing a target piece and melodic contour. By combining novelty search and objective based fitness, the system explores the harmonic space more thoroughly, while identifying novel harmonic progressions with desirable aesthetics.

Our results indicate that, while the generated harmonic progressions may not be 100% perfect (as this depends on the specific musical corpus used, input melody, and target piece), they may be good enough for music composition and performance tasks. For instance, we have found that the harmonic space of 371 J.S. Bach Chorales, used herein, is rich with novel aesthetic possibilities, possibilities that the grand master himself never realized.

The Harmonic Navigator may be used to explore compositional ideas in harmonic spaces derived from various musical corpora. Additionally, it may be used to revitalize traditional classroom training in tonal harmony via tonal harmony games. Finally, it may be used in musical happenings, together with MIDI and OSC controllers, as well as traditional instruments, to create harmonic contexts for improvised performances.

Acknowledgements. This work has been supported in part by NSF (grants IIS-0736480, IIS-0849499 and IIS-1049554) and a donation from the Classical Music Archives. The authors would like to acknowledge Dana Hughes for correcting MIDI transcription errors in the 371-piece Riemenschneider corpus of Bach chorales. Also, Dana Hughes and Kenneth Hanson for their contributions to the custom Jython libraries used in this project.

References

1. Cope, D.: Virtual Music: Computer Synthesis of Musical Style. MIT Press, Cambridge (2004)
2. Eigenfeldt, A., Pasquier, P.: Realtime Generation of Harmonic Progressions Using Controlled Markov Selection. In: 1st International Conference on Computational Creativity (ICCC-X), pp. 16–25. ACM Press, New York (2010)
3. Legname, O.: Density Degree of Intervals and Chords. 20th Century Music 4(11), 8–14 (1997)
4. Lehman, J., Stanley, K.: Abandoning Objectives: Evolution through the Search for Novelty Alone. Evolutionary Computation Journal 19(2), 189–223 (2011)
5. Manaris, B., Romero, J., Machado, P., Krehbiel, D., Hirzel, T., Pharr, W., Davis, R.B.: Zipf's Law, Music Classification and Aesthetics. Computer Music Journal 29(1), 55–69 (2005)
6. Manaris, B., Roos, P., Machado, P., Krehbiel, D., Pellicoro, L., Romero, J.: A Corpus-Based Hybrid Approach to Music Analysis and Composition. In: 22nd Conference on Artificial Intelligence (AAAI 2007), pp. 839–845. AAAI Press, Palo Alto (2007)
7. Manaris, B., Hughes, D., Vassilandonakis, Y.: Monterey Mirror: Combining Markov Models, Genetic Algorithms, and Power Laws. In: 1st Workshop in Evolutionary Music, 2011 IEEE Congress on Evolutionary Computation (CEC 2011), pp. 33–40. IEEE Press, Piscataway (2011)
8. Manaris, B., Johnson, D., Vassilandonakis, Y.: Harmonic Navigator: A Gesture-Driven, Corpus-Based Approach to Music Analysis, Composition, and Performance. In: 2nd International Workshop on Musical Metacreation (MUME 2013), 9th AAAI Conference on Artificial Intelligence and Interactive Digital Entertainment, pp. 67–74. AAAI Press, Palo Alto (2013)
9. Johnson, D., Manaris, B., Vassilandonakis, Y.: Harmonic Navigator: An Innovative, Gesture-Driven User Interface for Exploring Harmonic Spaces in Musical Corpora. In: Kurosu, M. (ed.) HCI 2014, Part II. LNCS, vol. 8511, pp. 58–68. Springer, Heidelberg (2014)
10. Manaris, B., Roos, P., Krehbiel, D., Zalonis, T., Armstrong, J.R.: Zipf's Law, Power Laws and Music Aesthetics. In: Li, T., Ogihara, M., Tzanetakis, G. (eds.) Music Data Mining, pp. 169–216. CRC Press, Boca Raton (2011)
11. Pachet, F.: Beyond the Cybernetic Jam Fantasy: The Continuator. IEEE Computer Graphics and Applications 24(1), 31–35 (2004)
12. Rosen, C.: The Classical Style; Haydn, Mozart, Beethoven, p. 26. W.W. Norton & Co., New York (1971)
13. Schoenberg, A.: Structural Functions of Harmony, pp. 192–196. W.W. Norton & Co., New York (1954)

Genomic: Evolving Sound Treatments Using Genetic Algorithms

Thomas M. Stoll

Dartmouth College, Bregman Music and Audio Research Studio,
Hanover, NH, USA
Thomas.M.Stoll@dartmouth.edu

Abstract. There are many systems for the evolution of creative musical
material, that create and/or manipulate musical score data or synthesis
parameters with a variety of techniques. This paper aims to add the technique of corpus-based sound sampling and processing to the list of applications used in conjunction with genetic algorithms. Genomic, a simple
system for evolving sound treatment parameters, is presented, along with
two simple use cases. Finally, a more complex process is outlined where
sound treatment parameters are evolved and stored in a database with
associated metadata for further organization and compositional use.

1 Motivation

The application of genetic and evolutionary algorithms to music composition
and creativity has been explored in considerable detail. Systems might be divided into categories based on the types of data that are used: numeric musical
notation, symbolic musical notation, usually in string or array form, and numerical synthesis parameters. With these genome-like simple representations as
input, complex "phenotypes" can be rendered, depending how the information
is translated. There are, however, fewer examples of methods using preexist-
ing audio data–sound files–directly. Genomic is software designed to explore the
intelligent synthesis of sound treatments, sound sequences, and sound corpora
using sampled audio files. Genomic is intended to work with sound as sound,
and, while mostly ignorant of symbolic constructs such as pitch and rhythm, is
based on comparing numerical measurements of timbre.

This paper reviews research directions most relevant to the application of evolutionary applications to sound treatments, and also provides a brief background
to corpus-based processing of audio and musical data, insofar as it is later applied to sound treatments. A basic method that uses a genetic algorithm (GA) to
evolve parameters for treatment of sound is outlined, along with corresponding
examples for evolving sound treatments, including discussions on the musical
goals of such systems. Finally, building upon this simple system, an approach
integrated within a simple corpus-based system is presented.

J. Romero et al. (Eds.): EvoMUSART 2014, LNCS 8601, pp. 107–118, 2014.

2   Past Work: Evolutionary Systems

Among the many examples of evolutionary systems that have been developed for manipulating musical parameters, there are artificial intelligence applications for sound creation that focus on sound design through sound synthesis algorithms, including applications for improvisation [3], large musical parameter spaces [2], cellular automata [5], and others [1].

Some researchers have focused on interactive genetic algorithms (IGAs). This development reflects the very real need to adapt tools for evolutionary creativity to the needs of composers and creators, who could incorporate such tools into their regular workflows. Johnson [9] describes an early IGA system with architecture, broadly-speaking, similar to Genomic. Similar to IGAs, co-evolutionary approaches allow the control parameters to change over time in a way that is adaptive to the dynamic nature of sonic utterance or musical performance. Although they have different goals, co-evolutionary systems, such as Casals' Frank [10], have inspired Genomic, especially regarding their approaches to improvisation.

Several researchers have made efforts to address evolution for creative purposes by situating an evolving agent in a system with other agents in a modeled ecosystem. McCormack and Bown [11] point out a common problem with evolutionary algorithms expected to produce creative output, implying that diversity of output is desired:

> Whereas standard evolutionary algorithms tend to converge to a single (sub)-optimum, niche construction can promote diversity and heterogeneity in an otherwise fixed and homogeneous evolutionary system. In systems where the design of an explicit fitness function may be difficult or impossible (as in many EMA [evolutionary music and art] systems), niche construction provides an alternate mechanism to explore a generative system's diversity over an IGA.

The ecosystem [12] analogy is intriguing and, as demonstrated below, the collection of a large number of treated sound files in conjunction with a simple corpus-backed system can be interpreted as a kind of ecosystem with a notion of diversity among a population of results. Although explained in the context of IGAs, Dahlstedt clearly explains the motivation and general process of exploring a musical parameter space, one that is "searched in shrinking steps, until an interesting target sound is found." [2] Included in this method for exploring parameter space is the requirement that exemplary individuals be saved for use in future generations.

Although focused on higher level spectral sound descriptors, Caetano and Rodet [6], introduce the idea of applying genetic algorithms to timbre interpolation with a focus on finding synthesis parameters that map to audible timbral transformations in resulting sounds. Their approach, in contrast to Genomic, relies on synthesis methods–source-filter synthesis[7]–with limited sets of parameters.

3   Genomic: An Evolutionary System for Sound Treatments

The simplest version of Genomic is software to manage a genetic algorithm that manipulates sound processing parameters for the treatment of some source sound. The majority of the code is Python, with a SuperCollider audio backend borrowed and adapted from CorpusDB[14]. Since there are only one or two sound files tracked in this example, there is no need to build a full database, although such a database is trivial to create. Genomic follows a traditional design pattern for genetic algorithms intended to evolve a set of input variables. Mel-frequency Cepstral Coefficients (MFCCs)–a common measure of timbre[8]–are used to characterize sounds within the database. Other analysis schemes may have similar potential.

3.1   A Note on Terminology

Throughout the article, the terms "sound treatment" and "sound processing" refer to the modification of a stored sound file by means of a specific ordering of audio signal processing routines. The space defined by all possible combinations of sound processing parameters is explored by the GA. The parameters for the genetic algorithm's genome, as explained below, are translated from genomic representation to sound synthesis parameters before carrying out the aforementioned audio signal processing.

3.2   Genotype and Phenotype

The genotype is simply a set of sound treatment parameters, distributed across stipulated ranges. Table 1 lists these parameters: three are gain stages, while the other four control comb filtering, clipping distortion, and spectral magnitude smearing. The parameter ranges were selected by hand so that the range of each parameter individually effects a reasonable amount of change in the resulting sound. In the current implementation, the signal processing chain is a series; other topologies and modular designs are possible, but beyond the scope of this paper.

Genes are represented as 8-bit integers derived from linearly interpolating the actual parameter ranges, so that the genetic algorithm can use binary representations of parameters that create phenotypes. Phenotypes, in this case, are simply the resulting audio from a process where a sound file is sampled and that sound is fed through processing or treatment stages, as outlined above. Audio is not necessarily stored to disc, although it can be for any individual. The analysis metadata–MFCCs per analysis frame–can also be seen as part of the phenotype, and this information is calculated and stored temporarily (or permanently) in the course of evolving a population(s).

3.3 Running the GA

The overall algorithm is outlined in the following list:

1. Sound synthesis parameters are initialized to random or default (see below) values for a pool of agents.
2. A single agent (in the first slot) is initialized to have parameters that correspond to no sound processing at all. This individual is created and analyzed once, as it will not change.
3. All modified sounds are generated and analyzed upon initialization. Their genotype data and resultant metadata are stored as the state of the system.
4. The system iterates through a series of generations.
5. Each generation includes opportunities for mutation using a crude aging process.
6. At the end of each generation, the most-fit individuals are mated, with their offspring replacing the least-fit.
7. Sounds may be recovered at the end of any generation by storing the sound file corresponding to an agent(s) *or by retaining metadata for reconstructing individual(s)*.
8. The process is stopped based on some stopping criteria, e.g. once some meta-analysis condition is met, or after a certain number of generations.

The population is seeded either with uniformly distributed random values, or with 0 values. Since the author decided that a genotype of "00000000" represents the case where no change to the sound is to occur, ranges of some parameters are inverted to this end. The mutation rate is the probability that a binary digit in a gene gets flipped each time that an age counter is incremented.

At certain intervals—every 20 generations, in this case, the population is ranked as to fitness and mating occurs. A certain number of individuals—20% of the total population, referred to as the margin—judged to be most and least fit are collected. The most fit are selected for mating with each other, and the offspring replace the least fit. In the mating process, genes are selected at random from each parent, forming the basis for a hybrid individual. It is possible that individuals are selected more than once for mating, since all selection is done with replacement.

Table 1. Seven sound parameters are manipulated in order to process sounds in Genomic

alpha	Gain scalar for unprocessed sound.
delay	Delay time for comb filtering.
decay	Decay time for comb filtering.
beta	Gain scalar for comb filter stage.
mult	Distortion multiplier that scales the signal before being clipped.
gamma	Gain scalar for distortion stage (post-distortion).
msbins	Spreads/smears energy across a specified number of bins.

3.4   The Fitness Function

In this simple system, similarity measurements are made by comparing analysis data per frame. By convention, sound is analyzed at a rate of 25 Hz. In the case where sounds have different lengths, the system truncates the longer sound file's time series data such that it contains an equal number of analysis time points as the shorter file. The system depends on the shorter file's duration to determine the resulting file's duration, which is a general limitation to the system. No attempt is made to reduce the complexity of the comparison by simplifying the analysis metadata, although this should be quite possible. In all cases, the metadata compared are the first 14 MFCCs. Other measures of timbre are quite possible, including higher MFCC dimensions. In the case of Genomic, and since the first coefficient of the MFCCs contains amplitude envelope information, we use this as a rough measure of sounds' overall shape. Accordingly, in our fitness function, we weight this amplitude-envelope matching equally to the comparison of higher (timbral) MFCC bins.

3.5   Implementation

The author's system relies on the creation of a large number of sound files that represent the current state of each individual in the pool of evolving agents. SuperCollider's non-real time (NRT) mode is used to take advantage of the fact that sounds can be rendered with custom parameterized sound designs, saved to disc, and analyzed in a fraction of the time it would take to render in a real time system. SuperCollider is also necessary, because of its unique capabilities for modular and programmable sound design. As mentioned above, each sound and processing combination can be reduced to a set of parameters; in this current version of the system, the sound design algorithm–the specific ordering of unit generators (UGens)–is fixed. The same synthesis object–a SuperCollider synthesis object (Synth)–contains sampling, processing, and analysis UGens:

```
chain = PlayBuf.ar(1, buffer_number, ...) * alpha;

chain = CombC.ar(chain, 2.0, c_delay, c_decay) * beta;
chain = (chain * d_mult).clip2(d_amp) * gamma;
chain = PV_MagSmear( FFT(LocalBuf(4096), chain), ms_bins);
chain = IFFT(chain);

mfccs = MFCC.kr(chain);
Logger.kr(mfccs, Impulse.kr( 1 / hop ), analysis_buffer_number);
```

The Python code deals only with metadata; it triggers synthesis through an operating system process, and reads the resulting data from a multi-channel WAV file that is created at the end of each analysis subprocess.

4   Goals for Evolution

The system, as described, will evolve novel sound transformations with no guidance from a user. The system has been tested with random and stationary initial values. Two evolutionary processes are attempted: one attempts to evolve processed sounds that are dissimilar to the original unprocessed sound; the other attempts to evolve processing for one sound such that it is transformed to be similar to some different (unmodified) target sound.

4.1   Evolving Novelty

Despite the simplicity of this evolutionary system, the result is a group of evolving sounds that follow decidedly non-random patterns of development, due to the nature of the genetic algorithm's ability to generate and test multiple solutions. Figure 1 shows the results of two separate runs evolving novel transformations based on the above parameterized Synth with different sounds and randomized initial values. Standard deviation values, showing the variance in the distances used in the fitness function, are included for illustration.

This pattern is typical, over a range of sounds, with populations gradually become more dissimilar from the original.

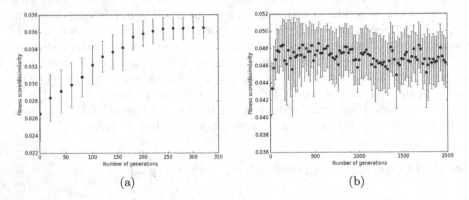

| | |
| (a) | (b) |

Fig. 1. In the first example, the average distance (dissimilarity) between all the pool sounds and the target sound reaches a stable value. In the second example, no stable value is found in 2000 generations.

The results of evolving transformations where individuals are seeded with parameters corresponding to no processing yield similar results; however, in these cases, overall average similarity trajectories start at zero. This case is more interesting from a musical perspective, as the resulting sounds from intermediate generations can perhaps be used to effect a series of more gradually changing sounds.

Clearly, something is happening here as the result of an evolutionary program, but the goal of the evolving system is not very well designed. The definition of the fitness function as a dissimilarity measure suggests the relative inadequacy of dissimilarity when guiding the selection of transformation parameters. As a metric, dissimilarity of data is not reliable, since there is no way to characterize *how* any given data is dissimilar, only *by how much*. Put another way, two separate sound transformations may count as similar distances measured from the target sounds, but these similar values actually represent two quite different results. The large number of data points (25 per second) used in the comparisons may yield a measurement with a level of detail too high (and therefore too noisy) to capture the general similarity of the sounds produced. Moreover, given the fact that four out of the seven parameters are gain stages, quite often results converge on individuals with noticeably higher or lower gain values in opposition to the loudness of the original. When hearing the results of this first poorly defined goal-directed task, this effect is often quite clear.

4.2   Evolving towards a Target

In contrast to the simplest case where the system evolves sound transformations that are increasingly less similar to an original, the targeted system is well-suited to evolve transformations of some sound **A** that are gradually more like some untreated sound **B**. The software code for this is nearly identical to the code for the previous section; the only difference is that we now have to track two separate unmodified sound files. The effect of this change of goal is dramatic. No longer do we rely on an ill-defined fitness goal. Now we are setting out with the goal of minimizing dissimilarity with the hope that our algorithm finds transformations that make some sound more similar to a target sound. There is no guarantee that our algorithm finds a transformation that exactly (or even closely) matches the target. This goal that is beyond the scope of this paper. Underlying this simple process is the notion of a sonic "analogical reasoning" [13], which has been identified as a central theme in AI creativity research.

As stated above, the system does not change in this case except to track multiple files. We run the same tests for this task, noting that the data now shows general progression toward higher similarity (lower distances between analysis data). Figures 2 and 3 show that we reach a stable state after a certain number of generations; the first example uses the same pair of sound files for the target sound and the pool of evolving transformed sounds, while the second example uses different sounds. There is an explicit stopping condition that determines the end of the evolutionary process based on the rate of change in average dissimilarity between population members and the target.

5   Extending Genomic with CorpusDB

A corpus-based system offers the opportunity to structure and store metadata for sequences of both sampled sound material as well as processing algorithms

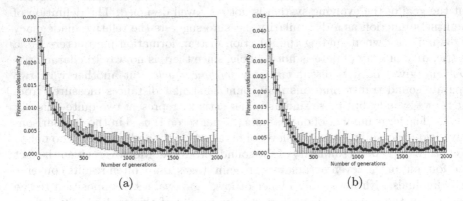

(a)   (b)

Fig. 2. In both examples, the average distance (dissimilarity) between all the population sounds and the target sound reaches a stable value–after more or less gradually diverging from the original

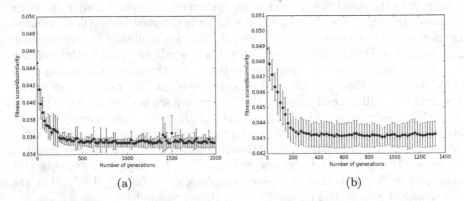

(a)   (b)

Fig. 3. The sound being modified is different than the target sound for the comparison. This shows the same basic pattern as when one file is used for both target and modification.

applied to transforming those sounds. CorpusDB [14], a set of Python classes that encapsulate many common functions for corpus-based processing, is a technique for managing large numbers of sounds and data about those sounds. The software represents sounds and sound transformation parameters in a tree structure and is uniquely suited for applications where there is a requirement that sound created through an evolutionary process be saved and recovered. Corpora developed for Genomic consist of one, two, or more sound file nodes, and hundreds of child nodes corresponding to modified sounds. Analysis data for individual sounds are stored alongside parameters defining creation of the sounds.

Extending Genomic involves making a few simple extensions to the above system. The goal of this system is to use the genetic algorithm to populate a table with variants of sounds that have been evolved to be similar to other sounds in the table. An example scenario follows the following steps:

1. Several untreated target and original sound pairs are selected.
2. Each sound is added to the corpus.
3. The genetic algorithm is run multiple times for each target sound, with each of the other target sounds as seeds for the evolving sound transformations.
4. Subsets of sounds are selected randomly from the most fit individuals at the end of each run.
5. Each subset is added to a corpus corpus.

Intuitively, this process should, over some number of runs, create a series of sounds that are variants of unprocessed sounds modified to sound similar to other untreated sounds. Again, there is no guarantee of the relative quality of the matches, but CorpusDB allows for the storage of intermediate results, with analysis data and parameter sets stored for selected individuals at any point during the running of the GA. One may reseed and run the GA any number of times, preserving results in a separate corpus. This ability allows for another unique feature: the ability to run genetic algorithms for many generations, examine the exemplary results from each generation, analyze these results, and, finally, to return the variations which are, ideally, the most varied. The comparison of exemplary individuals from across runs of the GA is performed only after all the runs are complete.

5.1   Developing a Corpus from Several Seed Sounds

The above algorithm has been run with short (ca. 2 seconds) sound samples of a cymbal–bowed and struck–and a bowed viola. For each sound source-target pair, the algorithm is run for 100 generations, and the best 5 individuals are selected and added to the corpus every 10th generation. For three source sounds, the end result is a corpus populated by 6 * (100/10) * 5 = 300 individuals, each derived from a source-target pair, plus the three original individuals. The resulting corpus can then be analyzed for patterns within the set of derived sounds. Figure 4 shows an similarity matrix for a resulting corpus.

The fact that we can preserve the intermediate results of the genetic algorithm allows for another powerful tool: the ability to look for patterns in metadata from those steps in order to determine, after the fact, when the most likely individuals may have evolved. In Figure 5 we see the means and standard deviations of the fitness/dissimilarity function. As the population evolves, the average similarity does not strictly decrease over time, but rather exhibits small deviations as the genetic algorithm explores different areas. We can look to the generations where the mean is relatively stable and retrieve those individuals for further use, or we can even choose generations from which to pull individual results interactively.

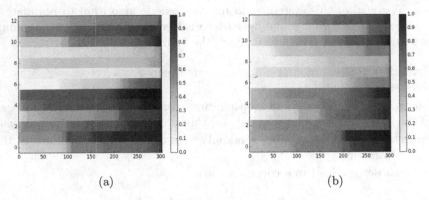

(a)   (b)

Fig. 4. MFCC analysis data for all members of a corpora formed by evolving parameters using all pairings of 3 source sounds. While there appears to be some overlap, this data shows the variation among evolved individuals.

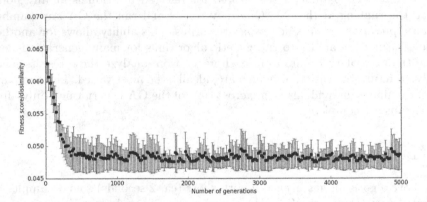

Fig. 5. Long-term population trends. There is the possibility that interesting individuals may be extracted from from generation 500 onward, since the population's mean does not settle.

5.2   Observations

A few interesting aspects of this process are observed. An open-ended evolutionary process, such as the one described above, likely benefits from a stopping condition for the automatic generation of the transformations. There is no reason why the first stable set of individuals would be the only viable results. In the examples in this paper, the number of generations is set to an arbitrary number. There is no reason why an open-ended run with many thousands of generations might not reveal additional results.

This paper makes no claims as to the feasibility of making meaningful timbral interpolations as in [6], but rather lays out a new way of using GAs to explore the space of potential sound transformations for any sound. It is hoped that additional analysis and control parameters will allow for finer tuning of the process, and it is expected that these processes are scalable to larger collections of sound material.

6   Conclusion and Future Work

This paper has presented a useful system for the evolution of sound processing treatments. Simple and moderately complex use cases were discussed that demonstrated the potential for Genomic to serve as an intelligent tool for selecting input sounds for a sound corpus.

There are a number of refinements that are possible. The use of CorpusDB for more detailed segmentation and analysis should simplify comparisons of material generated in the system. It should be possible to construct more complex–and more relevant–similarity schemes: for example, the use of a further analysis parameter(s) to guide comparison, the use of amplitude envelope comparisons, and the possibility that linear piecewise segmentation or dynamic time-warping (DTW) might be used to compare sounds of different durations. There is also the possibility to develop and evolve weights for distance calculations based on multidimensional data.

The author will continue to develop strategies to deal with comparing similar sounds as sequential multidimensional data: resampling techniques, learning weights for the analysis stages, dynamic time warping, etc. Eventually, the approach outlined in this paper should be amenable to development of a full, robust ecosystem backing intelligent semi-autonomous management of sound resources.

Acknowledgements and Audio Links. Software code–Python and SuperCollider, audio examples, and further information may be obtained at the author's web site: `www.tomstoll.net`. The author would like to thank the reviewers for their detailed and insightful comments.

References

1. Miranda, E.R., Biles, A. (eds.): Evolutionary Computer Music. Springer (2007)
2. Dahlstedt, P.: Evolution in Creative Sound Design. In: Evolutionary Computer Music, pp. 79–99. Springer (2007)
3. Biles, J.: GenJam: A genetic algorithm for generating jazz solos. In: Proceedings of the International Computer Music Conference, pp. 131–137 (1994)
4. Dahlstedt, P.: Creating and exploring huge parameter spaces: interactive evolution as a tool for sound generation. In: Proceedings of the 2001 International Computer Music Conference, pp. 235–242 (2001)
5. Miranda, E.R.: Evolving cellular automata music: From sound synthesis to composition. In: Proceedings of the 2001 Workshop on Artificial Life Models for Musical Applications (2001)

6. Caetano, M., Rodet, X.: Independent manipulation of high-level spectral envelope shape features for sound morphing by means of evolutionary computation. In: Proceedings of the 13th International Conference on Digital Audio Effects (DAFx), vol. 21 (2010)
7. Arfib, D., Keiler, F., Zölzer, U.: Source-filter processing. DAFX: Digital Audio Effects, 279–329 (2002)
8. Terasawa, H., Slaney, M., Berger, J.: Perceptual distance in timbre space. In: Proceedings of the International Conference on Auditory Display (ICAD 2005), pp. 61–68 (2005)
9. Johnson, C.: Exploring the sound-space of synthesis algorithms using interactive genetic algorithms. In: Proceedings of the AISB 1999 Symposium on Musical Creativity, pp. 20–27 (1999)
10. Casals, D.P.: Remembering the future: genetic co-evolution and MPEG7 matching in the creation of artificial music improvisors. Ph.D. Thesis, University of East Anglia (2008)
11. McCormack, J., Bown, O.: Life?s What You Make: Niche Construction and Evolutionary Art Applications of Evolutionary Computing, 528–537 (2009)
12. McCormack, J.: Evolving Sonic Ecosystems. Kybercetes 32(1/2), 184–202 (2003)
13. Goel, A.: Design, Analogy, and Creativity. IEEE Expert 12(3), 62–70 (1997)
14. Stoll, T.: CorpusDB: Software for Analysis, Storage, and Manipulation of Sound Corpora. Ninth Artificial Intelligence and Interactive Digital Entertainment Conference (2013)

Evolving an Aircraft
Using a Parametric Design System

Jonathan Byrne, Philip Cardiff, Anthony Brabazon and Michael O'Neill

Natural Computing Research & Applications Group
University College Dublin, Ireland
jonathanbyrn@gmail.com, {philip.cardiff,anthony.brabazon,m.oneill}@ucd.ie

Abstract. Traditional CAD tools generate a static solution to a design problem. Parametric systems allow the user to explore many variations on that design theme. Such systems make the computer a generative design tool and are already used extensively as a rapid prototyping technique in architecture and aeronautics. Combining a design generation tool with an evolutionary algorithm provides a methodology for optimising designs. This works uses NASA's parametric aircraft design tool (OpenVSP) and an evolutionary algorithm to evolve a range of aircraft that maximise lift and reduce drag while remaining within the framework of the original design. Our approach allows the designer to automatically optimise their chosen design and to generate models with improved aerodynamic efficiency.

1 Introduction

Parametric systems are changing the conceptual design process in the same way spreadsheets changed finance. Both operate on the same principle. The user defines the relationships in a system and then changes variables in that system to rapidly explore alternative possibilities. Instead of manually creating a CAD model by dragging and dropping components, the parametric design is specified using variables and functions. Just as changing the value in a cell causes the spreadsheet to recalculate all related values, changing a variable that defines part of a model will adapt all the connected components so as to maintain a coherent design. Although there is a longer lead time to implement the initial model, once it is encoded the user can easily create endless variations on the original.

Evolutionary algorithms (EA) have shown their ability to optimise the shape and form of designs [11, 1]. One of the primary considerations when applying an evolutionary algorithm to a design problem is the representation used. The representation limits the search space by defining all the designs the algorithm could possibly generate. Poor representations generate designs that are invalid (internal faces, unconnected parts), infeasible (wrong scale) or missing the desired functionality. Creating a suitable representation is a difficult task that requires knowledge of both programming and of the specific domain.

J. Romero et al. (Eds.): EvoMUSART 2014, LNCS 8601, pp. 119–130, 2014.

Parametric systems provide a novel solution to the representation problem. A well implemented parametric system will only generate valid designs and incorporates domain knowledge. It also allows a designer with no formal programming experience to define the representation for the evolutionary algorithm. The designer provides the initial model and specifies the range limits so as to generate appropriate variations of their design. Parametric models make evolutionary optimisation directly accessible to the designer and allows them to use their domain knowledge to create a representation that generates feasible designs.

This work combines NASA's parametric aircraft system (OpenVSP) and a computational fluid dynamics solver (OpenFOAM) with an evolutionary algorithm to generate a variety of optimised and novel designs. Sect. 2 gives an overview of parametric design systems and their application in industry. Sect. 3 describes the fluid dynamics solver used to generate the fitness values for the model. Sect. 4 discusses previous aircraft optimisation examples that used evolutionary approaches. Sect. 5 describes the parametric blended wing body model that was used and the two experiments that were carried out. Finally sections 6 and 7 examine the results of the experiments and the conclusions that can be drawn from them.

2   Parametric Design

Parametric design defines the relationships between components in a design. Generating a model consisting of hierarchical and geometric relations allows for exploration of possible variations on the initial design while still limiting the search space. Instead of manually placing and connecting components as is done in traditional CAD, component generating algorithms are linked with user definable variables. Defining the relationship between the components prevents invalid design generation. A change to one component will automatically effect a change on any connected component.

Parametric systems traditionally consist of basic components tailored for a particular design problem. An example of this would be the wing, fuselage and engine components in OpenVSP. Pre-defined components allow for domain knowledge to be embedded in the software and simplifies the design process. Although the user can explicitly define design components by programming them, normally model creation is done by combining existing components using a graphical interface. Many parametric design systems, such as grasshopper [5], are implemented using a drag and drop interface, shown in Fig. 1. The user can then manipulate the input and evaluate the benefit of the component to the overall design. An important aspect of parametric design is that the user observes the effects caused by manipulating a variable in real time, allowing the user to treat the underlying algorithm as a black box. Showing the effect of changing input to the system means that the user does not require an understanding of the underlying mechanics of the system, but instead gives them an intuitive understanding of how the components in a system are related to each other.

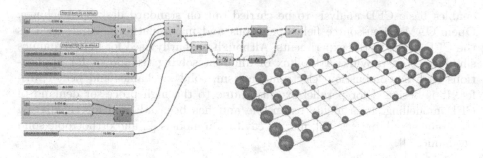

Fig. 1. The GUI for the Grasshopper parametric system. The variables are shown in the purple boxes on the left and are connected to the shape generating functions. The output design is on the right.

Parametric design tools have now been introduced into mainstream design software. There is the Grasshopper parametric design tool plug-in for the Rhino modelling system [5], Bentley Systems have implemented a program called Generative Components [23] based on the parametric design paradigm and Dassault Systems have developed CATIA, a CAD system combined with a parametric design tool. Parametric functionality was introduced to AutoCAD 2010 to allow for algorithmic manipulation of a design.

Combining parametric systems with structural analysis allows the user to make informed decisions about the geometric alterations during the conceptual design stage [9]. EIFForm is a parametric design system that optimises lattice structures by using structural analysis and a simulated annealing algorithm. The results have been used to design a structure in the inner courtyard of Schindler house [20]. Bollinger et al. [3] have developed parametric design systems that incorporate structural considerations and have used it to generate roofing structures for the BMW Welt Museum, Munich and the Rolex learning centre, EPFL, Lausanne. CATIA was combined with GSA structural analysis software [22] to evolve roofing structures for a football stadium [9].

The software used in this work is open vehicle sketch pad (OpenVSP). It was originally developed by NASA and Sterling Software as a rapid geometry modeler for conceptual aircraft [8] and has since developed into a stand-alone aircraft modelling tool. It was released as open-source software in 2012 under the NASA open source agreement. This work combines aerodynamic analysis with OpenVSP to analyse the lift and drag of the models. The next section discusses how the aerodynamic analysis was performed and the solver that was used.

3   Computational Fluid Dynamics

Computational Fluid Dynamics (CFD) uses numerical methods to solve how liquids and gases interact with surfaces. Although the calculations are computationally intensive, the dramatic increase in the power of standard hardware enables basic CFD analysis to be carried out on standard desktop machines. OpenFOAM (open-source field operations and manipulation) [24] is used as the CFD solver in the experiments. Although primarily used for fluid dynamics simulations, it provides a toolbox of different solving techniques for applications such as combustion, electromagnetism, solid mechanics and heat transfer. It is designed for parallel execution due to the high processor demand of CFD modelling. It is highly extensible and has been adapted for calculating transonic aerodynamics [25], marine cavitation models [2] and orthotropic solid mechanics [4].

Fig. 2. The relative wind velocity and turbulence caused by the blended wing body model

The solver used in the experiments is the semi-implicit method for pressure linked equations (SIMPLE) algorithm [17]. It is a steady state numerical solver for efficiently solving the Navier-Stokes equations that describe fluid motion. The algorithm forms the basis of CFD software and has been adopted to calculate the transfer of mass and momentum in a discretised three dimensional environment. The solver iteratively calculates the pressure and velocity within the system. Post processing then calculates the lift and drag forces generated by the model and these are used as the fitness value.

4   Evolutionary Aircraft Optimisation

"Since design problems defy comprehensive description and offer an inexhaustible number of solutions the design process cannot have a finite and identifiable end. The designer's job is never really done and it is probably always possible to do better." [13].

Design problems inevitably involve some trade off between desirable attributes [21]. In aircraft design there is a trade off between lift and drag which is known as aerodynamic efficiency. A design must have a minimal cross-sectional area to reduce drag but it must also have a large wing to maximise lift. Conflicting objectives mean there is no one perfect solution, instead there is a pareto front of equally viable designs. Multi-objective problems are difficult to optimise but the population based approach of evolutionary algorithms has been shown to be a successful approach [26]. Multi-objective evolutionary algorithms (MOEA) have been shown to be a useful approach for finding the best compromise when tackling a multi-objective problem [6].

Accordingly there have been several MOEA approaches to evolving aerodynamically efficient aircraft. Due to the computational expense of CFD analysis most approaches focus on 2D optimisation of airfoils [18, 1, 14]. Different components have been optimised individually, such as the wing [15] or the turbine blade positions [19]. Although some large scale optimisation examples have been carried out [7, 16] the difficulty in defining such a complex representation has limited its application. The next section describes the aircraft model that is the basis for optimisation and the multi-objective algorithm used to optimise the aerodynamic efficiency.

5   Optimisation of Blended Wing Body Design

In traditional aircraft the fuselage provides little or no lift to the craft. Originally developed by NASA, the blended wing body (BWB) flattened the fuselage into the shape of an airfoil so that the entire craft generated lift. The BWB model has been used extensively as a test case for Multidisciplinary design optimisation (MDO) [12]. MDO uses optimisation techniques to solve design problems that span multiple disciplines. A parametric model of the BWB is provided with OpenVSP and was used as a test case. The model is shown in Fig. 3. One of the main advantages of parametric design optimisation is that it is easy to optimise specific features of a design. In order to highlight this two separate experiments were carried out. The first experiment solely optimised the airfoils while maintaining the predefined shape, so as to improve the design while remaining visually the same. The second experiment varied the sections and airfoils of wing structure, allowing the algorithm to explore different design possibilities.

The initial experiment only allows variation of the airfoil sections of the wing. The airfoil is defined by a National Advisory Committee for Aeronautics (NACA) profile system [10]. The NACA profile combines mean lines and thickness distribution to obtain the desired airfoil shapes. The NACA system allows the airfoil to be defined using only three parameters: thickness, camber and camber location. The wing on the BWB consists of 3 distinct wing sections. Only the camber and thickness were varied while the camber location remained fixed. Fixing the camber location of the airfoils means that the overall shape and configuration of the aircraft remain close to the original model.

The second experiment increases the number of variables in the representation to include the span, sweep, tip chord, root chord and dihedral angle of the wing. These features of the wing are illustrated in Fig. 6. Although changing this many features means that the model will vary greatly from the original design, it examines if the optimiser can be used as an explorative tool. Increasing

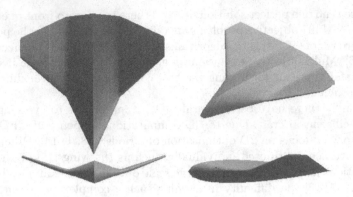

Fig. 3. The blended wing body model

```
<aircraft>  ::= <foil0><foil1><foil2>
<airfoil>   ::= {'Camber':<r>, 'Thickness':<r>}
<foil0>     ::= self.plane['foil0'] = <airfoil>
<foil1>     ::= self.plane['foil1'] = <airfoil>
<foil2>     ::= self.plane['foil2'] = <airfoil>
<r>         ::= 0.<digit><digit><digit><digit><digit>
<digit>     ::= 1|2|3|4|5|6|7|8|9|0
```

Fig. 4. The encoding used to describe the camber and thickness of each airfoil on the wing

the amount of variability in the representation will generate more infeasible design but does open up the possibility of finding an improved yet unexpected configuration.

5.1 Experimental Settings

A standard genetic algorithm (GA) was used in the experiments. The settings used by the GA are shown in Table 1. Both lift and drag are being used as fitness values to evaluate the designs. In order to evolve designs that incorporated these features, the non-sorting genetic algorithm II (NSGA2) multi-objective fitness function was used for selection and replacement [6]. Multi-objective search algorithms do not assume there is a globally optimal solution but that there are a set of non-dominated solutions. The non-dominated solutions are solutions that are better than the rest of the population for at least a single constraint and at least equivalent for all other constraints. The NSGA2 algorithm selects the least dominated solutions to create the child population.

In order to evaluate the performance of the evolutionary algorithm, the results were compared against randomly generated designs from the search space, essentially a brute force approach. This comparison examines if any useful genetic information is being transferred between individuals and whether the parametric

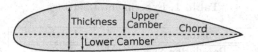

Fig. 5. NACA profile of an airfoil

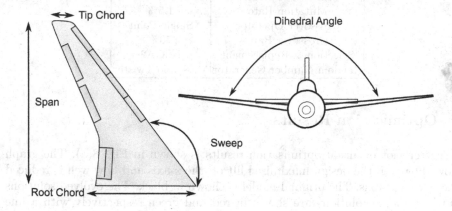

Fig. 6. The features of a wing section

```
<aircraft>  ::= <section0><section1><foil0><foil1><foil2>
<section>   ::= {'Span':<r>, 'TC':<r>,'RC':<r>,'Sweep':<r>,'Dihedral':<r>}
<airfoil>   ::= {'Camber':<r>, 'Thickness':<r>}
<section0>  ::= self.plane['section0'] = <section>
<section1>  ::= self.plane['section1'] = <section>
<foil0>     ::= self.plane['foil0'] = <airfoil>
<foil1>     ::= self.plane['foil1'] = <airfoil>
<foil2>     ::= self.plane['foil2'] = <airfoil>
<r>         ::= 0.<digit><digit><digit><digit><digit>
<digit>     ::= 1|2|3|4|5|6|7|8|9|0
```

Fig. 7. The encoding used to vary each section and airfoil of the wing

representation is amenable to evolutionary search. Due to limited available computing power only two runs were carried out for each experiment. Although this does not constitute a sufficient sample size to support the efficacy of stochastic methods such as an EA, the intention of these experiments is to examine if the aerodynamic efficiency of a pre-specified model could be optimised. As such the pareto-efficiency of the individuals in the final population will be used to judge the effectiveness of the algorithm as an active design tool.

Table 1. Experimental Settings

Property	Setting
Population Size	50
Generations	50
No. of Runs	2
Mutation Operator	Per Codon
Mutation Rate	1.5%
Crossover Operator	Single Point
Crossover Rate	70%
Selection & Replacement	NSGA2
Random Number Generator	Mersenne Twister

6   Optimisation Results

A scatter plot of airfoil optimisation results is shown in Fig. 8(a). The graph shows how well the design maximised lift on the x-axis and how well it reduced drag on the y-axis. The original model is shown in black. The evolved solutions and brute force solutions are shown in red and green respectively with a line connecting individuals on the pareto front. Overall the pareto front of the evolved solutions is equivalent to the randomly generated solutions, indicating that no benefit was provided by the genetic information.

That an evolutionary approach did not outperform a brute force approach could be the result of the constrained nature of the representation. Each of the three airfoil sections had two variables. Although each individual was encoded by thirty integers, the range of each variable was limited to viable designs. Such a constrained representation could generate good solutions by random variation. This conclusion would be supported by the fact that both approaches generated

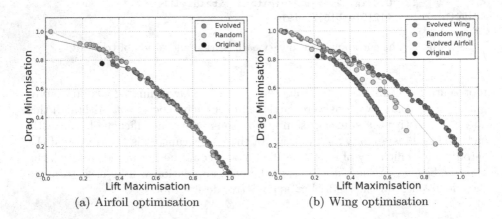

(a) Airfoil optimisation   (b) Wing optimisation

Fig. 8. The Pareto front for the final generation of aircraft. The results from the airfoil optimisation are shown in blue in the wing optimisation for comparison.

Fig. 9. Airfoil optimisation in order of increasing lift. The overall shape of the design remains the same.

pareto optimal designs that outperformed the original model. A sample of individuals from the pareto front are shown in Fig. 9. Limiting the evolvable representation to the airfoils produced optimised solutions that maintained the same overall design as the BWB aircraft.

A scatter plot of wing and airfoil optimisation are shown in Fig. 8(b). Again the original model is shown in black and the evolved and brute force solutions are shown in red and green respectively. The graph shows how well the design maximised lift on the x-axis and how well it reduced drag on the y-axis. The increased variability of the representation greatly increased the range of the Pareto fronts when compared to the airfoil optimisation results, shown in blue.

The evolved Pareto front is distinct from the brute force approach. The randomly generated individuals tend to cluster around minimal drag designs as it is easy to find a design with a smaller wing, all the individual has to do is reduce the size of the aircraft. It is more difficult to find a design with an aerodynamically viable wing and this is where the evolutionary algorithm excels.

This result is highlighted by examining the average population fitness during the course of a run, as shown in Fig. 10. The NSGA2 selection operator compares child and adult populations so the graphs start at the second generation. The evolutionary algorithm is already populated with high fitness designs at this point while the selection pressure quickly improves average fitness of the brute force approach up to a point. In both drag and lift graphs the brute force approach plateaus after five generations. The evolutionary approach on the other hand continues to improve lift (while sacrificing drag efficiency) for the duration of the run.

A sample of the individuals on the pareto front are shown in Fig. 11. The relaxing of the evolvable representation resulted in many different wing configurations being generated. The amount of variation shows that such design problems are highly open-ended with no single optimal design configuration. It also suggests that allowing the algorithm to evolve more components of the representation could result in novel yet highly efficient designs.

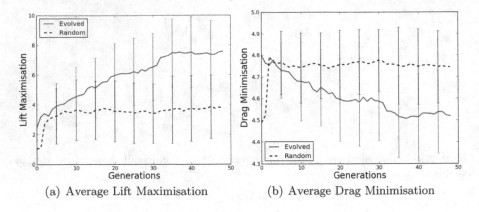

(a) Average Lift Maximisation   (b) Average Drag Minimisation

Fig. 10. The change in average lift/drag during the course of the run

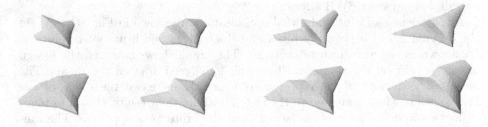

Fig. 11. Wing optimisation in order of increasing lift. The increased number of variables resulted in different wing configurations.

7   Conclusions

A parametric system allows the designer, not the programmer, to specify the design to be evolved. The experiments showed that the level of design optimisation could be varied. Specific components of the model can be optimised or the model can be used as the basis for generating entirely different aircraft configurations. Although the sample size of the experiment is too small to draw any significant conclusions, initial results indicate that this representation is capable of being optimised. Even in experiment where brute force approaches performed comparably to evolutionary approaches, both generated designs that outperformed the original parametric model. This approach could potentially be applied to any existing parametric design to generate optimised solutions, turning the computer into an active design tool in the conceptual design process.

Acknowledgments. We would like to thank Science Foundation Ireland, the Financial Mathematics Computation Cluster and Andrea McMahon for her help during this project. We also wish to acknowledge the DJEI/DES/SFI/HEA Irish Centre for High-End Computing (ICHEC) for the provision of computational facilities and support. This work was funded by the SFI grants 08/RFP/CMS1115, 08/IN.1/I1868 and 08/SRC/FM1389.

References

[1] Alpman, E.: Airfoil shape optimization using evolutionary algorithms. Aerospace Engineering Department, Pennstate University (2004)

[2] Bensow, R.E., Bark, G.: Simulating cavitating flows with les in openfoam. In: V European Conference on Computational Fluid Dynamics, pp. 14–17 (2010)

[3] Bollinger, K., Grohmann, M., Tessman, O.: Form, force, performance: Multi-parametric structural design. Architectural Design 78(2), 20–25 (2008)

[4] Cardiff, P., Karač, A., Ivanković, A.: A large strain finite volume method for orthotropic bodies with general material orientations. In: Computer Methods in Applied Mechanics and Engineering (2013)

[5] Day, M.: Grasshopper, generative modelling (2010),
http://www.grasshopper3d.com/

[6] Deb, K., Pratap, A., Agarwal, S., Meyarivan, T.: A fast and elitist multiobjective genetic algorithm: NSGA-II. IEEE Transactions on Evolutionary Computation 6(2), 182–197 (2002) ISSN 1089-778X

[7] Dulikravich, G.S.: Aerodynamic shape design and optimization-status and trends. Journal of Aircraft 29(6), 1020–1026 (1992)

[8] Gloudemans, J.R., Davis, P.C., Gelhausen, P.A.: A rapid geometry modeler for conceptual aircraft. In: 34th Aerospace Sciences Meeting and Exhibit, Reno, NV, January, pp. 15–18 (1996)

[9] Holzer, D., Hough, R., Burry, M.: Parametric design and structural optimisation for early design exploration. International Journal of Architectural Computing 5(4), 625–643 (2007)

[10] Jacobs, E.N., Ward, K.E., Pinkerton, R.M.: The characteristics of 78 related airfoil sections from tests in the variable-density wind tunnel. Technical report, DTIC Document (1933)

[11] Kicinger, R., Arciszewski, T., De Jong, K.: Evolutionary computation and structural design: A survey of the state-of-the-art. Computers and Structures 83(23-24), 1943–1978 (2005), ISSN 0045-7949, doi: 10.1016/j.compstruc.2005.03.002

[12] Andy Ko, Y.-Y.: The multidisciplinary design optimization of a distributed propulsion blended-wing-body aircraft. PhD thesis, Virginia Polytechnic Institute and State University (2003)

[13] Lawson, B.: How designers think: the design process demystified. Elsevier/Architectural (2006), ISBN 9780750660778,
http://books.google.ie/books?id=1PvqZJNAdG8C

[14] Naujoks, B., Willmes, L., Haase, W., Bäck, T., Schütz, M.: Multi-point airfoil optimization using evolution strategies. In: Proc. European Congress on Computational Methods in Applied Sciences and Engineering (ECCOMAS 2000)(CD-Rom and Book of Abstracts), p. 948 (2000)

[15] Obayashi, S.: Multidisciplinary design optimization of aircraft wing planform based on evolutionary algorithms. In: 1998 IEEE International Conference on Systems, Man, and Cybernetics, vol. 4, pp. 3148–3153. IEEE (1998)

[16] Parmee, I.C., Watson, A.H.: Preliminary airframe design using co-evolutionary multiobjective genetic algorithms. In: Proceedings of the Genetic and Evolutionary Computation Conference, vol. 2, pp. 1657–1665 (1999)

[17] Patankar, S.V., Spalding, D.B.: A calculation procedure for heat, mass and momentum transfer in three-dimensional parabolic flows. International Journal of Heat and Mass Transfer 15(10), 1787–1806 (1972), http://www.sciencedirect.com/science/article/pii/0017931072900543, doi: http://dx.doi.org/10.1016/0017-9310(72)90054-3, ISSN 0017-9310

[18] Quagliarella, D., D'ambrosio, D., Iollo, A.: Airfoil design using navier-stokes equations and hybrid evolutionary optimization techniques. Technical report, DTIC Document (2003)

[19] Rogalsky, T., Derksen, R.W., Kocabiyik, S.: An aerodynamic design technique for optimizing fan blade spacing. In: Proceedings of the 7th Annual Conference of the Computational Fluid Dynamics Society of Canada, pp. 2–29. Citeseer (1999)

[20] Shea, K., Aish, R., Gourtovaia, M.: Towards integrated performance-driven generative design tools. Automation in Construction 14(2), 253–264 (2005) ISSN 0926-5805

[21] Simon, H.A.: The sciences of the artificial. The MIT Press (1996)

[22] Oasys Software. GSA, structural analysis version 8.5 (2011), http://www.oasys-software.com/gsa-analysis.html

[23] Bentley Sytems. Generative components, v8i (2011), http://www.bentley.com/getgc/

[24] Weller, H.G., Tabor, G., Jasak, H., Fureby, C.: A tensorial approach to computational continuum mechanics using object-oriented techniques. Computers in physics 12, 620 (1998)

[25] Wüthrich, B., Lee, Y.: Simulation and validation of compressible flow in nozzle geometries and validation of OpenFOAM for this application. PhD thesis, ETH, Swiss Federal Institute of Technology Zurich, Institute of Fluid Dynamics (2007)

[26] Zitzler, E., Thiele, L.: Multiobjective evolutionary algorithms: a comparative case study and the strength Pareto approach. IEEE Trans. Evolutionary Computation 3(4), 257–271 (1999)

Author Index

Abreu, Pedro H.   13
Amaro, Hugo   13

Bishop, Andrew   62
Brabazon, Anthony   119
Byrne, Jonathan   119

Carballal, Adrian   50, 74
Cardiff, Philip   119
Castro, Luz   50, 74
Ciesielski, Vic   62
Costelloe, Dan   38

Eisenmann, Jonathan   1

Greenfield, Gary   85

Johnson, David   95

Lewis, Matthew   1

Machado, Penousal   13
Manaris, Bill   95
Martins, Tiago   13
McCormack, Jon   26

Nicolau, Miguel   38

O'Neill, Michael   119

Parent, Rick   1
Perez, Rebeca   50, 74

Santos, Antonino   50, 74
Stoll, Thomas M.   107

Trist, Karen   62

Vassilandonakis, Yiorgos   95